HURRICA
SQUADRONS

OF WORLD WAR II

IN FOCUS

RED
KITE

First published 2003 by
Red Kite
PO Box 223,
Walton on Thames
Surrey, KT12 3YQ

Designed by
Simon W Parry

Printed in Britain by
Ebenezer Baylis.

ISBN 0-9538061-5-4

Introduction

The Hawker Hurricane has generally been considered a second class fighter when compared with the Supermarine Spitfire. Maybe this was connected with the personalities and image of the respective chief designers, Camm being somewhat low key publicly and Mitchell achieving some publicity from a feature film following his untimely and sad death soon after the Spitfire took to the air. The Hurricane was certainly slower but its traditional construction made it more robust and pleasant to fly. In the Battle of France, where the Hurricane was the only RAF single-seat day fighter, when enemy pilots were shot down and survived they even claimed it was a Spitfire which had caused their premature return to earth. Without the Hurricane there would not have been a practical combat aircraft equipping the RAF for the Battle of France.

In the Battle of Britain, although Spitfire squadrons were becoming more plentiful, the Hurricane was still numerically the most common aircraft and the pilots made a considerable contribution to the Battle. This was not only in 11 Group in the Southeast of England, but also throughout Britain, even when squadrons were "resting" before rejoining the front line around London. It was not just the new inexperienced pilots who were lost in the Battles of France and Britain, but also flight and squadron commanders, showing that anyone was vulnerable in the confusion of combat. To not recognise the achievements of the Hurricane pilots throughout WW2 is a great disservice to their bravery, achievements and sacrifice.

Because Hurricanes also served with many squadrons and allied air forces in the Mediterranean, North Africa, Middle East and Asia, it has not been possible to fit them all into the format of this book. For this reason, Volume 1 deals with the Battles of France and Britain, and Volume 2 is planned to cover the remainder of the RAF, FAA and Allied Hurricane Squadrons in Focus. Where squadrons were equipped with Hurricanes for operation in France and Britain, the illustrations and data have included any subsequent overseas service for completeness. The only foreign air force to be covered in this account is Belgium, as its demise was so much part of the initial Battle of France.

It has not been possible to illustrate every Hurricane squadron, as some only operated the aircraft for a short period and others were very camera shy, particularly the second line units which were undertaking more mundane, but important tasks.

Philip J Birtles, Stevenage, September 2002.

Bibliography

Aces High - Shores & Williams
Battle of Britain - Len Deighton
Coastal Support & Special Squadrons of the RAF, & their Aircraft - John D R Rawlings.
Fighter Squadrons of the RAF & their Aircraft - John D R Rawlings
Hurricane, The Illustrated History - Philip J Birtles
Men of the Battle of Britain - Kenneth G. Wynn
RAF Serial logs - James J. Halley
Squadron Codes - Bowyer & Rawlings

Cover picture: **No. 3 Squadron's Hurricane Mk.IIcs in late 1941.**

Previous page: **Hurricanes of No. 32 Squadrons during a pre-war air display.**

Facing Page: **Canadian fitter Corporal Trimble of No. 401 Squadron checks out the instrument panel of one of the Hurricanes.**

CONTENTS

Prototype

HURRICANE

Dimensions:
Span 40'
Length 31' 6"
Height 13' 6"
Engine:
Rolls Royce Merlin C. 1,025hp, twelve cylinder V water cooled.
Armament:
Nil.
Performance:
312 mph, ceiling 33,000', range 500 miles

Above: **Hurricane Prototype K5083 in natural metal and silver finish with fabric covered wings, tail and rear fuselage. The aircraft flew for a short while with tailplane struts, but these were soon removed as unnecessary.**

Hurricane Prototype K5083. Ordered under contract 357483/34 to Air Ministry Specification F.36/34 it made its maiden flight from Brooklands on 6 November 1935 in the hands of George Bulman, the Chief Test Pilot with Hawker Aircraft, within a year of the first issue of manufacturing drawings. The Hurricane was a single seat low-wing monoplane day fighter armed with eight wing mounted Browning machine guns. Power came from a single Rolls-Royce PV-12 engine in the 1,000hp class, later to become the Merlin, driving a fixed pitch Watts wooden two-blade propeller. The primary structure was metal with initially fabric covered wings and tail surfaces and the rear fuselage was fabric covered over wooden fairings. Start of manufacturing drawings was made in May 1934 with the official order placed for an unarmed prototype on 21 February 1935.

The prototype completed its basic airworthiness tests with Hawker and was ready for the service evaluation at A&AEE Martlesham Heath from 7 February 1936, the major problem being the unreliability of the Merlin I engine, later corrected by designing a new cylinder head for the Merlin II. The first production contract for 600 aircraft was placed on 3 June 1936 and on 27 June the name Hurricane was approved. Although testing of the prototype was restricted due to delays with the Merlin IIs, it was used for aerodynamic development including spinning trials.

Further trials were flown at A&AEE Martlesham Heath, RAE Farnborough and Rolls-Royce Hucknall until 1937. Eight gun wings were fitted and flown on 17 August 1936

Below: **The prototype Hurricane K5083 at Brooklands featuring the fixed pitch wooden Watts propeller and original exhausts. It is also fitted with the original canopy, later replaced with one featuring more frames. (BAe)**

Mk.I

HURRICANE

Dimensions:
Span 40'
Length 31' 4"
Height 13'

Engine:
Rolls Royce Merlin II or III. 1,030hp, twelve cylinder V water cooled.

Performance:
Speed 335 mph, ceiling 36,000' range 525 miles.

Armament:
Eight 0.303 inch machine guns in wings.

Left: **Hurricane Mk.I L1648 from the first production batch of 600 aircraft was delivered to No. 85 Squadron at Debden in September 1938. It was wrecked when it overshot on landing on 6 October 1938.**

Below: **Hurricane Mk.I L1669 powered by a Rolls-Royce Merlin II developing 1,030hp at Martlesham Heath in 1939 prior to despatch to Khartoum for tropical trials. The aircraft later flew operationally, but was wrecked on 30 September 1940.**

Mk.IIa

HURRICANE

Dimensions:
Span 40'
Length 32' 21/4"
Height 13' 2"
Engine:
Rolls Royce Merlin XX. 1,185hp, twelve cylinder V water cooled.
Armament:
Eight 0.303 inch machine guns in wings.
Performance:
Speed 340 mph, ceiling 41,000', range 468 miles

Above: **Hurricane IIa Z3451 in March 1942 with underwing racks fitted for the carriage of bombs. This was one of a batch of 1,000 Hawker built Mk.IIs powered by Rolls Royce Merlin XX driving a de Havilland or Rotol three-blade variable pitch propeller.**

Right and below: **A study of Hurricane IIa, Series 2, Z2521 from the fifth production batch as it came off the Hawker production line. It was armed with eight machine guns and had the lengthened nose. (HSA)**

Mk.IIb

HURRICANE

Dimensions:
Span 40'
Length 32' 21/4"
Height 13' 2"

Engine:
Rolls Royce Merlin XX. 1,185hp, twelve cylinder V water cooled.

Armament:
Six, eight, or twelve 0.303 inch machine guns in wings. Two 250 or 500lb bombs.

Performance:
Speed 320 mph, ceiling 33,000', range 460 miles

Above: **Hurricane IIb BE485, AE-W, of No. 402 Squadron RCAF based at Warmwell carrying a pair of 250lb underwing bombs.**

Below: Glamour on the factory floor. Not a typical scene perhaps, but it does afford a good view of the construction and internal details of the Hurricane.

Mk.IIc

HURRICANE

Dimensions:
Span 40'
Length 32' 21/4"
Height 13' 2"

Engine:
Rolls Royce Merlin XX. 1,185hp, twelve cylinder V water cooled.

Armament:
Four 20mm Cannons in wings. Two 250 or 500lb bombs.

Performance:
Speed 334 mph, ceiling 36,000', range 460 miles

Above: **Hurricane IIc Z3888 fitted with a pair of 44 gallon underwing tanks which were more widely used than the 88 gallon tanks.**

Right: **Hurricane IIc prototype Z2905 in February 1942 fitted with a pair of 88 gallon underwing ferry tanks for long range deployments overseas. This aircraft features the four wing mounted 20mm cannons protruding from the leading edge which were used effectively in the ground attack role.**

Right: **Hurricane IIc HW603, named 'Our John' was one of three Hurricanes presented to the RAF by the mother of Wing Commander John Gillan DFC AFC. Gillan had been killed in action on 29 August 1941 in a Spitfire while leading the North Weald Wing on a fighter sweep. (ww2images.com)**

Mk.IId

GROUND ATTACK HURRICANE

Dimensions:
Span 40'
Length 32' 21/4"
Height 13' 2"

Engine:
Rolls Royce Merlin XX. 1,185hp, twelve cylinder V water cooled.

Armament:
Two 40mm cannons and two 0.303 machine guns in wings.

Performance:
Speed 332 mph, ceiling 32,100', range 420 miles

Above: **Hurricane IId HW719 fitted with a pair of 40mm Vickers anti-armour guns under the wings which was delivered to No.1 School of Specialised Low Attack at Milfield in January 1943.**

Below: **Hurricane IId KZ320 on the airfield at Langley where most of the Hurricanes were built during World War 2. This aircraft is fitted with a pair of Vickers underwing mounted 40mm anti-tank guns. (BAe)**

Mk.IV

GROUND ATTACK HURRICANE

Dimensions:
Span 40'
Length 32' 21/4"
Height 13' 2"
Engine:
Rolls Royce Merlin 24/27. 1,620hp, twelve cylinder V water cooled.
Armament:
Four 20mm or two 40mm cannons. Eight rocket projectiles or two bombs.
Performance:
Speed 280 mph, ceiling 29,100', range 450 miles

Above: **Hurricane Z2326 was originally built as a Mk.II, and later converted to the Mk.IV prototype armed with a pair of 40mm Vickers cannons with the fairings removed.**

Below: **Hurricane Mk.IV KZ198 with two underwing mounted Vickers 40mm anti-armour cannons and a tropicalised Merlin 27 driving a Rotol RS.5/11 four-blade propeller. (HSA)**

Mk.V

GROUND ATTACK HURRICANE

Dimensions:
Span 40'
Length 32' 21/4"
Height 13' 2"

Engine:
Rolls Royce Merlin 27. 1,635hp, twelve cylinder V water cooled.

Armament:
Four 20mm or two 40mm cannons. Eight rocket projectiles or two bombs.

Performance:
Speed 280 mph, ceiling 29,100', range 450 miles

Above: **Hurricane Mk.V KZ193 in November 1943, one of only two built fitted with a pair of underwing Vickers 40mm cannons. After performance trials at Brooklands it was converted to a Mk.IV and issued to No. 164 Squadron at Warmwell for shipping strikes from July 1943.**

Below: **Hurricane KX405 was built as a tropical Mk.IV and converted to a Mk.V prototype powered by a Merlin 32 engine driving a four-blade propeller. This version was designed for low level ground attack in hot climates and was fitted with additional armour plating. This aircraft was used for trials at Langley with Hawker and A&AEE Boscombe Down. It was later converted back to the Mk.IV configuration. (HSA)**

Mk.X

CANADIAN MK.1
HURRICANE

Dimensions:
Span 40'
Length 3' 4"
Height 13'

Engine:
Packard Merlin 28. 1,300hp, twelve cylinder V water cooled.

Armament:
Eight 0.303 machine guns.

Performance:
Speed 330 mph, ceiling 35,000'

Above: **Hurricane Mk.X AG111 of the Fighter Leaders School. The Canadian aircraft were built to a similar standard to the UK variants, but adapted for local conditions and equipment.**

Above: **Canadian Hurricane Mk.I 328 with the Test & Development Flight at RCAF Rockcliffe, Ontario on 28 August 1939. The first Canadian built Hurricane made its maiden flight on 10 January 1940. (Public Archives of Canada)**

Above:**Hurricane Mk.X AG122 was used by Rolls-Royce for Packard Merlin engine development driving a Hamilton Standard three blade variable pitch propeller. (BAe)**

Below: **RCAF Hurricane Mk.XII at Rockcliffe on 16 September 1942. A total of 1,451 Hurricanes were built in Canada by the Canadian Car & Foundry Company, shared between the RCAF for home defence, and the RAF for operations in the UK and overseas. (Public Archives of Canada)**

THE SQUADRONS

1 SQUADRON

Code Letters:
NA & JX

Usage:
Mk.I
Oct 38 to Apr 41
Mk.IIa
Feb to June 41
Mk. IIc
July 41 to Sept 42
Mk.1
Apr 42 to July 42
Mk. IIb
June 42 to Sept 42

Bases:
Tangmere 2/27 – 9/39
Northern France 9/39 – 6/41
Northolt 6/40
Tangmere 6/40 – 8/40
Northolt 8/40 – 9/40
Wittering 9/40 – 12/40
Northolt 12/40 – 1/41
Kenley 1/41 – 4/41
Croydon 4/41 – 5/41
Redhill 5/41 – 6.41
Kenley 6/41
Redhill 6/41 – 7/41
Tangmere 7/41 – 7/42
Acklington 7/42 – 2/43
Re-equipped with Typhoons.

Above: **Hurricane 1 L1681 of No. 1 Squadron with the fixed pitch two blade Watts wooden propeller and the original rudder without the ventral extension. This aircraft was lost in the Battle of France in May 1940. (W Huntley)**

Right: **Armourers re-load the 20mm cannons on a No. 1 Squadron Hurricane wearing the JX code letters. The symbols under the cockpit show three trains and one aircraft destroyed. (ww2images.com)**

Pilot Officer J F D Elkington

John Francis Durham Elkington was born in 1920 and went to Cranwell in 1939. In July 1940 he was posted to No. 1 Squadron then based at Tangmere. On 15 August he made a claim for an Me109 shot down into the sea. In another combat over Thorney Island on 16 August his Hurricane, P3173, was hit by fire from an Me109 and Elkington was forced to bale out injured. He stayed with the squadron until April 1941when he was posted away and saw no more combat. He left the RAF in 1975 as a Wing Commander.

Squadron Leader J F Demozay DSO DFC

French born Jean-Francois Demozay was a pre-war civilian pilot and began the war as an interpreter with No. 1 Squadron, but could not be evacuated with it. He commandeered a Bombay transport and flew it, with fifteen soldiers aboard, to England. After training as a fighter pilot he went back to No. 1 Squadron, later moving to Nos. 242 and 91 Squadrons. By the end of the war he was credited with 18 aircraft destroyed and 11 others damaged or probable. He died in a flying accident in December 1945.

Above: **Hurricane Mk.IIcs of No. 1 Squadron practice formation flying. (ww2images.com)**

Flight Lieutenant Karel Kuttelwascher

Czech born Kuttelwascher escaped to France in June 1939. He flew with the Armee de l'Air and came to England on the fall of France. Posted to No. 1 Squadron in October 1940, he flew several sweeps in 1941 before becoming a specialist night fighter pilot ending the war with 18 aircraft destroyed. After the war he returned home, but came back to England where he died in 1959.

Flight Lieutenant John Ignatius Kilmartin

'Killy' was born in Eire in 1913 and was shipped to Australia in 1922. After a time in China he joined the RAF and was posted to No. 43 Squadron and then to No. 1 Squadron in France. He claimed at least 10 victories over France before returning to England. After another spell with 43, during which he made two more claims, he took a variety of commands and staff jobs until he retired in 1958.

Right: **Squadron Leader A V Clowes DFC DFM climbs into his well worn Hurricane Mk. I. P3395 JX-B of No. 1 Squadron in a blast pen at Wittering during a rest from combat in the Battle of Britain. The wasp emblem used by Clowes is clearly visible below the exhausts. Also note worthy is the light coloured band around the spinner of the aircraft in the distance.**

1 RCAF SQUADRON

Code Letters:

YO

Usage:

Mk.I
June 40 to Mar 41

Bases:

Middle Wallop 6/40 – 7/40
Croydon 7/40 – 8/40
Northolt 8/40 - 10/40
Prestwick 10/40
Castletown 10/40 - 2/41
Digby 2/41 - 3/41
Re numbered 401 Squadron

Above: **A fitter works on one of the earliest Canadian Hurricanes fitted with a two blade prop and ring and bead sight. (ww2images.com)**

Squadron Leader Ernest Archibald McNab

McNab had joined the RCAF in 1926. He flew with the RCAF's aerobatic team, flew mail and did photo surveys. In 1937 he was in Briatin and was appointed a flight commander in No. 46 Squadron on an exchange attachment to the RAF. When war was declared he returned to Canada to take command of No. 1 Squadron (RCAF) and brought the squadron to Britain on 20 June 1940 with its own Canadian built Hurricanes. During the time that No. 1 Squadron (RCAF) was at Croydon, McNab flew with 111 Squadron to gain combat experience and destroyed a Do 17 on 15 August. During the Battle of Britain he destroyed three further aircraft with one shared, one probable and three more damaged. He was awarded the DFC and promoted to Wing Commander in October. In November 1940 he took a staff post in London and later returned to Canada.

Above: **Flying Officer Peter Lochnan joined the squadron on 30 August 1940. He brought down three aircraft, but was killed in a flying accident with No. 400 Squadron in May 1941.**

Above: **Original members of the squadron, Beverley Christmas (left) and W P Sprenger. Christmas survived the war, but Sprenger was killed in an accident on 26 November 1940.**

Flight Lieutenant Gordon Roy McGregor

McGregor was born on 1901 and, like McNab, was an accomplished pre-war airman. He was a flight commander when No. 1 Squadron arrived in Britain and brought down five aircraft with a further two probables and five damaged. He took over from McNab as Commanding Officer in November, but left to lead No. 402 Squadron (RCAF) in March 1941. He later held a number of posts and ended the war as the oldest Canadian fighter pilot of WW2.

Flying Officer Blair Dalzell Russel

Russel was a salesman before joining the RCAF and completed his training in May 1940. He took to air combat and brought down or damaged eleven aircraft in the Battle of Britain. In 1941 he returned to Canada, but was back in Britain in 1943 when he commanded No. 411 Squadron and became Wing Leader of 127 Wing. In May 1944 he demoted himself to Squadron Leader to lead No. 442 Squadron which was part of 'Johnnie' Johnson's Wing.

Below: **No. 1 Squadron RCAF at Northolt on 12 September 1940. Front row L-R: F/O Peterson, F/O Sprenger, S/L McNab, F/O Beardmore, F/O Nesbitt, F/O Christmas. Back row L-R: F/L Pollock, F/O Trevena, F/O Briese, F/O Pitcher, F/O Lochnan, F/L Reyno, F/O Blaiklock, F/O Norris, F/O Yuile, Capt Rankin.**

3

SQUADRON

Code Letters:

OP & QO

Usage:

Mk.I
March 38 to May 38
May 39 to Apr 41
Mk.IIb
Apr 41 to Oct 41
Mk.IIc
Apr 41 to Feb 43

Bases:

Kenley 8/36 – 5/39
Biggin Hill 5/39 – 9/39
Croydon 9/39 – 12/39
Hawkinge 12/39 – 1/40
Kenley 1/40 – 5/40
Merville 5/40
Kenley 5/40
Wick 5/40 – 9/40
Castletown 9/40
Turnhouse 9/40 – 10/40
Castletown 10/40 – 1/41
Skeabrae 1/41 – 2/41
Castletown 2/41 – 4/41
Martlesham Heath 4/41 – 6/41
Stapleford 6/41 – 8/41
Hunsdon 8/41 – 5/43

Re-equipped with Typhoons

Above: **L1934 in a pre-war marking scheme with a roundel on the port wing only. Following the initial re-equipment from Gladiators in March 1938 to Hurricanes at Kenley, the airfield was found to be too small and a temporary return was made to Gladiators until moving to Biggin Hill in May 1939 when it was issued again with Hurricanes. (ww2images.com)**

Right: **A pair of early Hurricane Mk.Is share the hangar at Kenley with Gladiators which they replaced for a short while.**

Below: **No. 3 Squadron Hurricane Mk.Is at Kenley with the pilots preparing for the Empire Air Day display in 1938 before the airfield was enlarged to better cope with the new low wing monoplane fighters.**

Above: **A lovely atmospheric photograph of QO-J with five more of No. 3 Squadron's Hurricanes flying into the sunset. (ww2images.com)**

Below: **The squadron moved to Martlesham Heath in April 1941, re-equipping with Hurricane IIs for the night defence of London, it later worked unsuccessfully with Turbinlite Havocs. Note the anti exhaust glare shield on the cowl.**

17 SQUADRON

Code Letters:

UV & YB

Usage:

Mk.I
June 39 to Feb 41
Mk.IIa
Feb 41 to Apr 41
Jan 42 to June 42
Mk.IIb
July 41 to Nov 41
June 42 to Aug 42
Mk.IIc
Aug 42 to June 44

Bases:

North Weald 5/39 – 9/39
Croydon 9/39
Debden 9/39 – 12/39
Martlesham 12/39 – 5/40
Hawkinge 5/40
Debden 5/40
Kenley 5/40 – 6/40
Le Mans, Dinard
& Jersey 6/40
Debden 6/40 – 8/40
Tangmere 8/40 – 9/40
Debden 9/40 – 10/40
Martlesham 10/40 – 2/41
Croydon 2/41 – 3/41
Martlesham 3/41 – 4/41
Castletown 4/41 – 6/41
Elgin 6/41 – 8/41
Dyce 8/41
Elgin 8/41 – 9/41
Tain 9/41 – 10/41
Catterick 10/41 – 11/41
To Asia 11/41 – 1/42, Burma, India & Singapore.

Above: **Stuck in North Weald's mud a small army of men man-handle a UV coded aircraft. The machine carries black and white wing undersides. (ww2images.com)**

Above right: **Hurricane I with No. 17 Squadron at North Weald in 1938 undergoing routine maintenance in the open and the squadron letters being painted on the fuselage. No. 17 Squadron changed to the YB code in September 1939. (Crown)**

Right: **P3878 YB-W with Pilot Officer Wissler. Wissler was killed on 11 November 1940 over the Thames Estuary engaging one of the last Stuka raids over Britain. P3878 was shot down off Chatham on 24 September 1940 its pilot, Pilot Officer Bird-Wilson, escaped with serious burns (Crown)**

Above: **Hawker built Hurricane Mk.I N2359 at Debden in August 1940. Right to left are Pilot Officer Stevens, LAC Jaquest - flight rigger and LAC McEvoy - flight mechanic all of 17 Squadron. The magnificent artwork depicts a winged Popeye with a screwdriver. The aircraft served with two OTU units before being written off in 1941. Leonard Stevens, from Hindhead in Surrey, flew throughout the Battle of Britain before moving to No. 145 Squadron as B Flight Commander in March 1941. On 21 May 1941 he collided with his number two over Tangmere and was killed in the resulting crash.**

Above: **A souvenir snap of a royal visit to No. 17 Squadron in the Spring of 1941.**

Right: **Hurricane I P2754, YB-W after a forced landing at Debden on 27 June 1940.**

32
SQUADRON

Code Letters:
KT & GZ

Usage:
Mk.I
Oct 38 to July 41
Mk.IIb
July 41 to Sep 42
Mk.IIc
Nov 41 to Aug 43

Bases:
Biggin Hill 9/32 – 1/40
Gravesend 1/40 – 3/40
Manston 3/40
Gravesend 3/40
Biggin Hill 3/40 – 5/40
Wittering 5/40 – 6/40
Biggin Hill 6/40 – 8/40
Acklington 8/40 – 12/40
Middle Wallop 12/40 – 2/41
Ibsley 2/41 – 4/41
Pembrey 4/41 – 6/41
Angle 6/41 – 11/41
Manston 11/41 – 5/42
West Malling 5/41 – 6/42
Friston 6/41 – 7/42
West Malling 7/42 – 9/42
Honiley 9/42 – 10/42
Baginton 10/42 – 11/42
North Africa 12/42 – 8/43

Above: **No. 32 Squadron replaced its Gauntlets with Hurricanes at Biggin Hill in October 1938 and played a major part in the Battle of France and Battle of Britain with a rest period covering the night defence of Newcastle. On returning south at the end of 1940 the squadron was allotted to convoy patrols, night fighting and intruding. In September 1942, after supporting the Dieppe raid, the squadron was sent to North Africa.**

Right: **P3522 GZ-V of No. 32 Squadron ready for take-off from Hawkinge on 31 July 1940 for another sortie. The aircraft was damaged on 15 August, but was repaired and sent to No. 213 Squadron. It crashed into the cloud covered Yorkshire Moors on 10 January 1941.**

Above: **Pilots of No. 32 Squadron taken at Hawkinge in July 1940. They are, from left to right, P/O R F Smthye, P/O K R Gillman, P/O J E Proctor, F/Lt P M Brothers, P/O D H Grice, P/O P M Gardner, P/O A F Eckford. Gillman was killed on 25 August 1940, but all the others survived the war. (ww2images.com)**

Right: **In December 1942 No. 32 Squadron moved to North Africa to cover the fothcoming landings. In March 1943 snow and heavy rainfall turned the normal arid North African airfields into swamps. The bad weather did not stop operations. Hurricanes at Maison Blanche used metal runways for take-off and landing. The squadron began re-equipping with Spitfire Vcs in May 1943 with the last Hurricane operation on 27 July.**

TRAINING UNITS

Above: **As the Spitfires began to take over day fighter duties in larger numbers, battle weary aircraft went to the OTUs. This is Canadian built Hurricane Mk.X AG162, allocated to 55 OTU at Aston Down. (Crown)**

Below: **Some arrivals were unconventional, an example being this Mk.I L1926 which had served with Nos. 3 and 312 Squadrons before going to 55 OTU at Aston Down. It was written off after this landing accident at Ouston on 15 April 1941. (H Lees)**

New pilots would receive advanced flying training on Miles Masters or North American Harvards, passing on to group pools to make the basic flying conversion to the Hurricane. Many of the pilots in the early part of the Battle of Britain were joining squadrons with minimal hours on the type, having no idea how to use the aircraft as a fighting machine. The early production aircraft were also not representative of the front line aircraft, which were fitted with the new reflector gun-sight and variable pitch propeller.

During the early part of the war there were insufficient Hurricanes to spare to form formal training units. The squadrons themselves were responsible for training new pilots, usually after being withdrawn from the battle on a 'rest' posting. To help supplement the busy squadrons, station flights were formed with older Hurricanes to help provide vital experience on the operation of the aircraft before novice pilots were thrown into battle.

Right: **A flight of Hurricane Mk.Is of 55 OTU wearing the PA code.**

With the arrival of later marks of Hurricane in early 1940 there were sufficient numbers of the early aircraft available for issue to Operational Training Units (OTUs). The first was 5 OTU, established at Aston Down in February 1940, equipped with Hurricanes, Defiants and Blenheims. This was followed in March by 6 OTU at Sutton Bridge and 7 OTU at Hawarden. These OTUs were later renumbered 55, 56, and 57 OTU.

The Hurricanes equipping these training units started with redundant Hurricane Mk.Is with fabric covered wings and the fixed wooden two-blade Watts propeller, the trainees by then being given about 40 hours of conversion and taught basic combat tactics and operational procedures. Such was the shortage of pilots during the Battle of Britain, that many of the new arrivals had little more than 20 hours on the type, putting more pressure on the operational pilots. Hurricane operational training continued in Britain until 1944 when 55 OTU closed.

Right: **Hurricanes were also used for the training of air gunners in the heavy bomber force by presenting them with realistic targets to aim at. This Hurricane IIc was with 1661 Conversion Unit based at Lindholme in 1945.**

Right: **Hurricane IIa Z2487 wearing the codes FC-T which appeared on Kenley Station Flight aircraft in 1941. The aircraft had formerly served with No. 306 Squadron and later went on to serve with No. 32 Squadron, 9 Pilots Advanced Flying Unit, 59 OTU, and 56 OTU. It was stuck off charge in July 1944.**

43 SQUADRON

Code Letters:
NQ & FT

Usage:
Mk.I
Nov 38 to July 41
Sept 42 to Nov 42
Mk.IIb
Apr 41 to Sep 42
Mk.IIc
Nov 42 to Mar 43

Bases:
Tangmere 12/26 – 11/39
Acklington 11/39 – 2/40
Wick 2/40 – 5/40
Tangmere 5/40 – 7/40
Northolt 7/40 – 8/40
Tangmere 8/40 – 9/40
Usworth 9/40 – 12/40
Drem 12/40 – 10/41
Acklington 10/41 – 7/42
Tangmere 7/41 – 9/42
Kirton-in-Lindsey 9/42 – 10/42
To North Africa 10/42 – 11/42
Gibraltar 11/42
Maison Blanche 11/42 – 3/43

Above: **The Fury formation flight in January 1939. Many of the top pilots here featured prominently in the battles of 1940. Left to right they are: Sgt Hallowes, F/O Christie, Sgt Carey, F/O Kilmartin, F/O Rotheram, F/O Hull, S/Ldr Bain, F/Lt Rosier, F/O Simpson, F/O Folkes, F/O Cos, Sgt Berry. (ww2images.com)**

Right: **No. 43 Squadron's original Hurricanes at Tangmere in November 1938. They have the NQ code letters that were replaced by FT at the outbreak of war. (Crown)**

Below: **The victorious pilots with a trophy of their victories while based at Wick in early 1940. (ww2images.com)**

Below: **Another trophy, this one from an Edinburgh club. P/O Lister holds the squadron's Fighting Cocks emblem.**

Above: **Jim Hallowes late in the war as a Wing Commander.**

Above: **Peter Townsend on the left and Caesar Hull.**

Right: **Pilots early in 1940, from left to right, Sergeant Arbuthnot, Sergeant Plenderleith, Sergeant Hallowes DFM, Flying Officer Simpson DFC, Flight Lieutenant Townsend DFC, Pilot Officer Upton DFC.**

John Arbuthnot was posted to No. 1 Squadron during the Battle of France and to No. 229 Squadron during the Battle of Britain. He was killed in a flying accident on 4 February 1941 when his Hurricane crashed into the Mersey.

Robert Plenderleith was posted to No. 73 Squadron in May 1940 and survived the war to become a test pilot until the 1960s.

Right: **The *Fighting Cocks* at Wick, left to right, Sergeant J A Buck, Flying Officer C A 'Tony' Woods-Scawen, Flight Lieutenant C Hull DFC, Flying Officer Wilkinson, Sergeant G W Garton.**

James Buck was shot down over the Channel on 19 July 1940 and drowned. Tony Woods-Scawen was shot down on 2 September over Kent but baled out too low. Caesar Hull, a South African, became the commanding Officer on 31 August after Squadron Leader Badger had been lost. Hull was shot down and killed a week later. Geoffrey Garton was posted to No. 73 Squadron in May 1940 and survived the war.

Squadron Leader Thomas F Dalton-Morgan

Cardiff born Tom flew torpedo bombers before the war and was posted as B Flight Commander in June 1940. He was shot down and baled out on 13 August, but was soon back in action. He was shot down and crash landed with a wounded knee on 6 September. Following the loss of Squadron Leader Hull he took command of the squadron as it was moved north to recover from its losses. He left the squadron in January 1942 and rose to the rank of Group Captain, staying in the RAF until 1952.

He is credited with 14 aircraft destroyed, 3 shared, 1 probable and 4 damaged.

Squadron Leader D A R G L du Vivier

Belgian Leroy du Vivier flew with Belgian airforce and was shot down on 11 May 1940. He escaped to England and was posted to No. 43 Squadron in August 1940. He was shot down and baled out injured on 2 September. After a few months with No. 229 Squadron he was back with the Fighting Cocks to become a flight commander in April 1941 and commanding officer in January 1942. He ended the war in North Africa and served in the post war Belgian Airforce. He died in a motorbike accident in 1981.

He is credited with 3 aircraft destroyed, 2 shared, 2 probable and 1 damaged.

Left: **A rather worn night fighting Hurricane Mk. 1 'FT-K'. By the start of 1941 No. 43 Squadron was based at Drem to defend Scottish targets from attack. On March 13/14, 1941, the first heavy attack was made on Glasgow and Clydeside by nearly 250 bombers. The Hurricanes attemped to intercept the raiders, but failed to make a single contact.**

Left: **Four aces, from left to right they are Jim Hallowes DFC, DFM (17 destroyed), John Simpson DFC (9 destroyed), Peter Townsend (9 destroyed), Upton (9 destroyed).**

Peter Townsend left the squadron in May 1940 to take command of No. 85 Squadron and held other commands, but he is best known for his post war life. He became Equerry to King George VI in 1944 and spent eight years in the Royal Household. His name is also closely associated with Princess Margaret.

Right: **Sergeant Bierer by Hurricane IIc "Lothaire" of No. 43 Squadron. The aircraft is painted in an overall black finish for interim night fighter duties. The squadron returned to Tangmere in mid 1942 for intruder operations over France.**

Right: **Two of No. 43 Squadron's pilots with Hurricane IIc HV817 FT-C on arrival at Maison Blanche in November 1942. The squadron went to North Africa and exchanged its Hurricanes for Spitfire Vcs in March 1943.**

Below: **Flight Lieutenant Lister by Hurricane IIc fitted with a tropical filter and the *Fighting Cocks* insignia on the engine cowling at Maison Blanche.**

Below: **Hurricane IIcs of No. 43 Squadron lined up at Tangmere in August 1942 after the major threat against Britain was over, ready for departure to North Africa.**

46 SQUADRON

Code Letters:

RJ & PO

Usage:

Mk.I
March 39 to May 41

Bases:

Digby 11/37 – 11/39
Acklington 11/39 – 1/40
Digby 1/40 – 5/40
HMS Glorious 4/40
Norway 4/40 – 6/40
HMS Glorious 6/40
Digby 6/40 – 9/40
Stapleford 9/40 – 11/40
North Weald 11/40 – 12/40
Digby 12/40 – 2/41
Church Fenton 2/41 – 3/41
Sherburn-in-Elmet 3/41 – 5/41

Above: **A No. 46 Squadron Hurricane I, PO-C, being loaded aboard *HMS Glorious* at Greenock on 1 May 1940 bound for Norway. (Crown)**

The squadron exchanged Gauntlets for Hurricane Is in March 1939. In May 1940 the squadron's Hurricanes were lifted aboard *HMS Glorious* and delivered to Harstad in Norway to defend against the invading Germans. A move was made to Skaanland on 26 May, but on 8 June the order was made to evacuate. It was considered impossible to land aboard the carrier and the Hurricanes were ordered to be destroyed, but New Zealander Patrick Jameson (right) obtained permission to try the landing and succeeded. Unfortunately *Glorious* met the battleships *Scharnhorst* and *Gneisenau* and was sunk with the loss of most on board. Squadron Leader Cross and Flight Lieutenant Jameson were among the thirty or so survivors and held onto a Carley float for three days before being picked up by a Norwegian ship - by then only seven were alive and two more died on the journey to land. Jameson went on to survive the war and retired as a Group Captain in 1960.

Below: **The squadron re-formed at Digby. Here are pilots at Stapleford Abbotts in October 1940. They are, left to right, F/O Ambrose, 'Vinc' the intelligence officer, F/O Young, P/O Leggett, F.O McGregor, Sgt Earp, F/Lt Lefevre. (ww2images.com)**

Hurricane Mk.I, OP-D/L1934, No.3 Squadron. Topsides: Dark Earth, Dark Green. Undersides: Aluminium, White and Black. 25in Fuselage roundels, 35in upper roundels, Medium Sea Grey codes. Black serials. Page 20.

Hurricane Mk.I, YB-J/N2359, No.17 Squadron. Topsides: Dark Earth, Dark Green. Undersides: Sky. 49in Fuselage roundels. 49in Red/Blue upper roundels. Medium Sea Grey codes. Black serials. Page 68.

Hurricane Mk.I, DU-N/P3612, No.312 Squadron. Topsides: Dark Earth, Dark Green Undersides: Sky, with Black underside to port wing. 35in Fuselage roundels, 49in Red/Blue upper roundels, 45in underwing roundels. Sky fuselage band. Medium Sea Grey codes. Black serial. Czech insignia below cockpit. Page 75.

Hurricane Mk.I, RF-E/P3700, No.303 (Polish) Squadron. Topsides: Dark Green, Dark Earth. Undersides: Sky. 35in Fuselage roundels. 49in Red/Blue upper roundels. 45in Underwing roundels. Codes in Medium Sea Grey. Black serials. No.303 Squadron insignia beneath cockpit. Page 66.

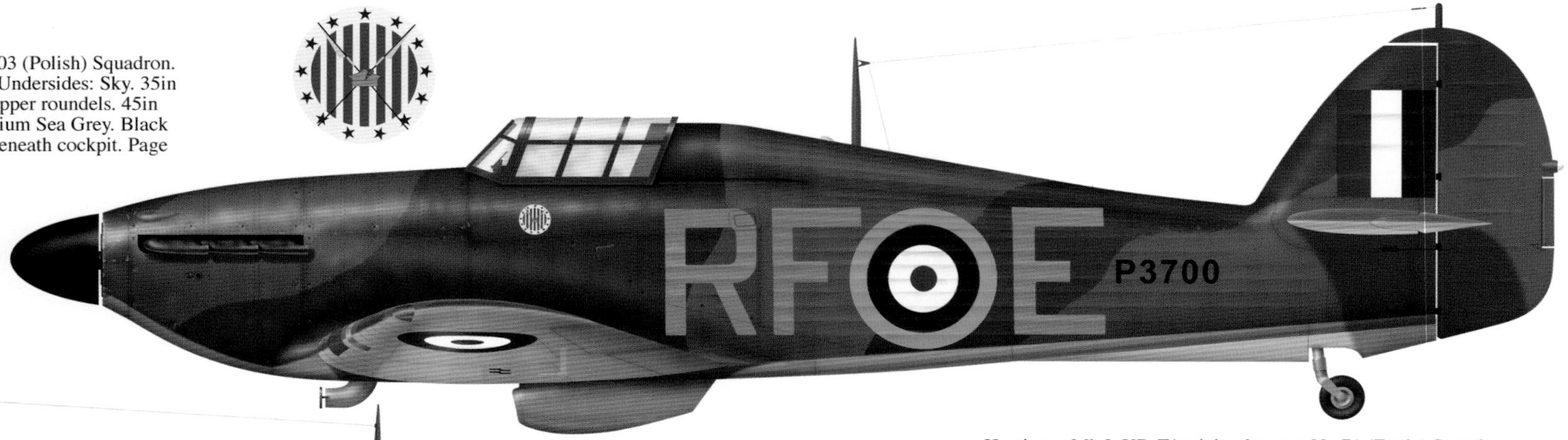

Hurricane Mk.I, XR-Z/serial unknown, No.71 (Eagle) Squadron. Topsides: Dark Green, Dark Earth, (nose colours are estimated from photographic reference). Undersides: Sky. 35in Fuselage roundels. 49in Red/Blue upper roundels. 45in Underwing roundels. Fuselage band in Sky. Page 35.

Hurricane Mk.I, VY-X/serial unknown, No.85 Squadron. Overall nocturnal finish of Night. 25in Fuselage roundels. 49in Red/Blue upper roundels. Codes in Medium Sea Grey. No.85 Squadron 'Hexagon' insignia carried beneath cockpit. Page 41.

Hurricane Mk.IIb, AE-W/BE485, No.402 Squadron, Royal Canadian Air Force. Topsides: Dark Green, Ocean Grey. Undersides: Medium Sea Grey. 35in Fuselage roundels, 49in Red/Blue upper roundels. 50in Underwing roundels. Codes in Sky. Sky fuselage band. Black serials. Note the two 250lb bombs carried underwing. Page 78.

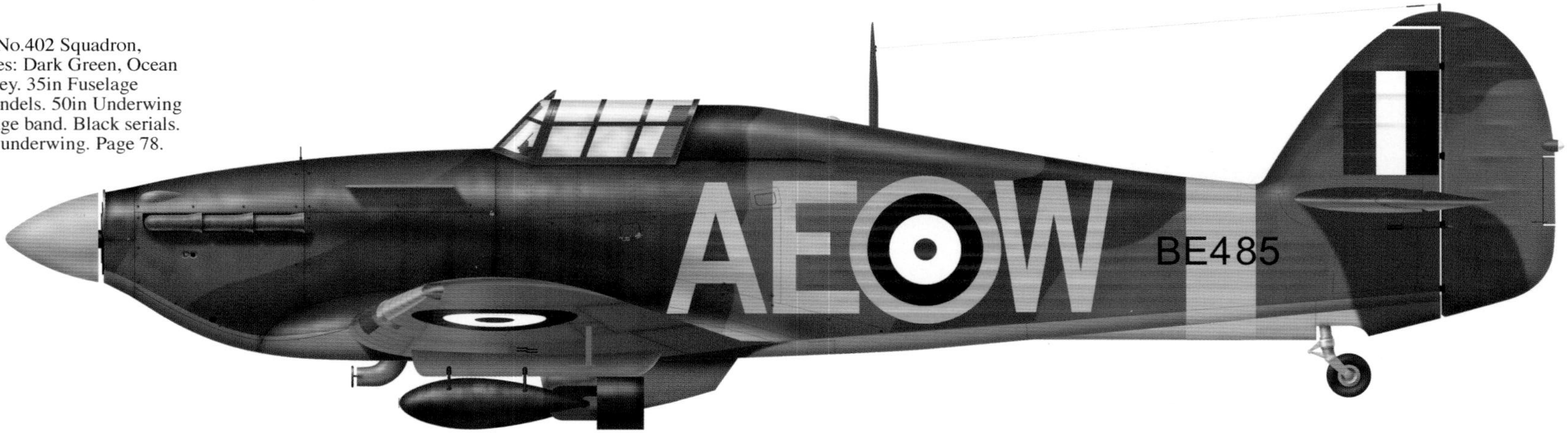

Hurricane Mk.IIb, 49-FK/Z3768, No.34 Squadron, 151 Wing. Topsides: Dark Green, Dark Earth. Undersides: Sky Blue. 35in Fuselage roundels. 49in Red/Blue upper roundels. 50in Underwing roundels. Codes possibly in Medium Sea Grey. Serials in Black. Page 51.

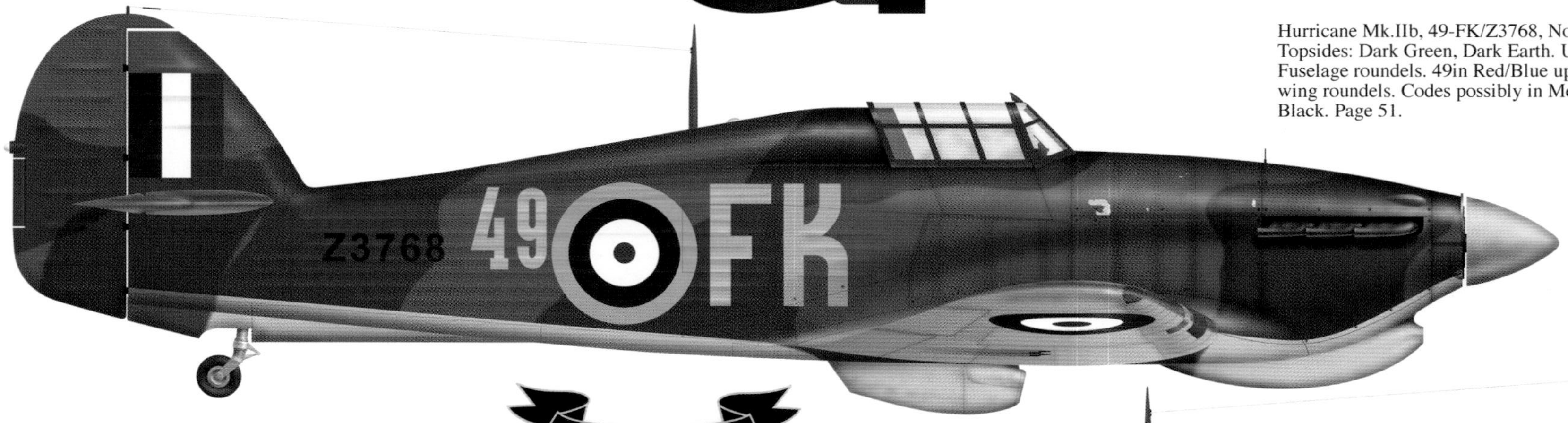

Hurricane Mk.IIc, LK-?/HL864, No.87 Squadron. Topsides: Dark Green, Ocean Grey. Undersides: Night nocturnal finish. 36in Fuselage roundels. 49in Red/Blue upper roundels. No underwing roundels. Codes and serials in Medium Sea Grey. Page 43.

Hurricane Mk.X, EH-W/AG162, No.55 OTU (Operational Training Unit), Aston Down. Upper surfaces: Dark Green and Ocean Grey. Undersides: Nocturnal finish of worn Night 36in fuselage roundels. 49in Red/Blue upper wing roundels. Codes in Sky. Black serials. Sky fuselage band. Page 26.

Hurricane Mk.X, HK-G/AG111, Fighter Leaders School, Millfield. Topsides: Dark Green and Ocean Grey. Undersides: Medium Sea Grey. Codes in Sky, with Black serials. Sky fuselage band. 36in fuselage roundels. 49in Red/Blue upper wing roundels. 32in underwing roundels. Page 14.

Hurricane Mk.IV, BP173, No.137 Squadron, used for rocket projectile trials, in July 1942. Topsides: Dark Green and Ocean Grey. Undersides in Medium Sea Grey. 36in fuselage roundels. 49in Red and Blue upper roundels. 32in underwing roundels. Eight 60lb rocket projectiles carried underwing. Page 52.

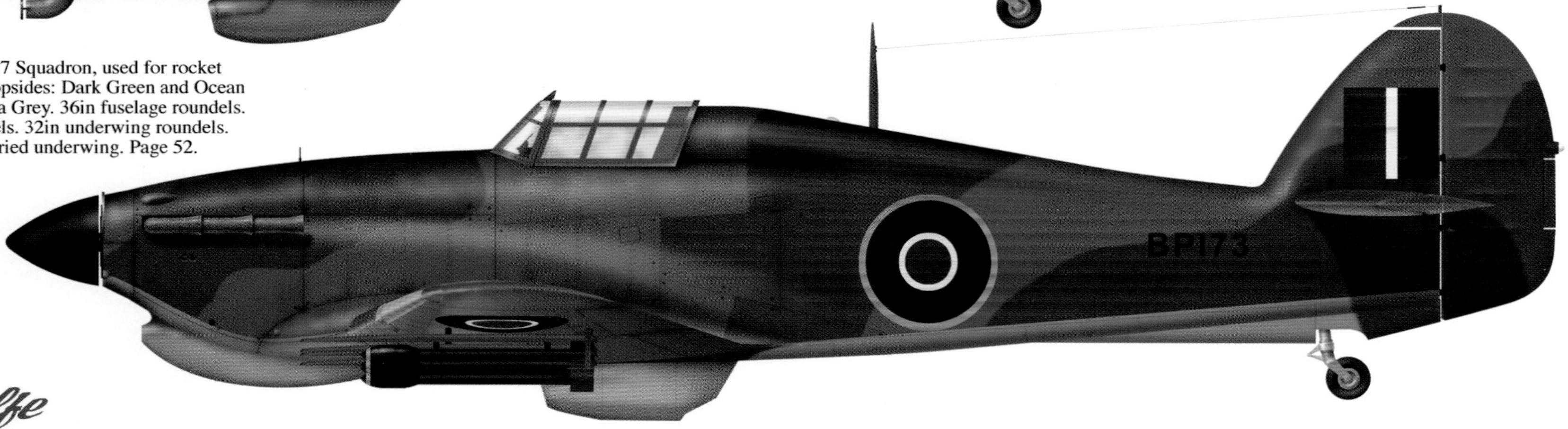

56 SQUADRON

Code Letters:

LR & US

Usage:

Mk.I
April 38 to Feb 41
Mk.IIb
Feb 41 to Mar 42

Bases:

North Weald 10/27 – 10/39
Martlesham Heath 10/39 – 2/40
North Weald 2/40 – 5/40
Digby 5/40 – 6/40
North Weald 6/40 – 9/40
Boscombe Down 9/40 – 11/40
Middle Wallop 11/40 – 12/40
North Weald 12/40 – 6/41
Martlesham Heath 6/41
Duxford 6/41 – 3/42

Above: **A formation of early Hurricane Is with 56 Squadron in 1939 with Watts two blade fixed pitch propellers and without the lower extension to the rudder. (Crown)**

Below: **Dated 17 August 1939, this terrific study of L1609 was taken during an exercise at North Weald. The aircraft went to Nos. 17, 501, 253 and 3 Squadrons before it was lost over France on 17 May 1940 when F/O Jones baled out.**

Two scenes showing No. 56 Squadron at North Weald in July 1940 before the height of the Battle of Britain.

63 SQUADRON

Code Letters:
UB

Usage:
Mk.IIc
Mar 44 to May 44
Sept 44 to Dec 44

Bases:
Turnhouse 1/44 – 4/44
Woodvale 4/44 – 5/44
North Weald 9/44 – 11/44
Manston 11/44
North Weald 11/44 – 1/45

Above: **In February 1944, No. 63 Squadron began practising combined operations in preparation for D-Day, mainly on tactical reconnaissance duties. The initial equipment was Mustangs, joined by Hurricanes, which were later replaced by Spitfires. These were used in action, spotting targets for naval bombardment. (ww2images.com)**

EAGLE SQUADRON

Formed at Church Fenton on 19 September 1940 as the first "Eagle" squadron with American volunteer pilots. The first action was on 17 April 1941 and the first confirmed victory was claimed by Pilot Officer Dunn with the destruction of a Bf 109f over Lille on 21 July. The Hurricanes were replaced by Spitfires in August and the squadron was transferred to the USAAC at Debden in September 1942.

Right: One of the original pilots, Flying Officer 'Red' Tobin, from Los Angeles.

71 EAGLE SQUADRON

Code Letters:
XR

Usage:
Mk.I
Nov 40 to May 41
Mk.IIa
May 41 to Aug 41

Bases:
Church Fenton 9/40 - 11.40
Kirton-in-Lindsey 11/40 – 4/41
Martlesham Heath 4/41 – 6/41
North Weald 6/41 – 12/41

Below: An unusual style of fuselage codes on XR-Z.

73 SQUADRON

Code Letters:

HV & TP

Usage:

Mk.I
July 38 to Jan 42
Mk.IIb
Oct 41 to Feb 42

Bases:

Digby 11/37 – 9/39
Northern France 9/39 – 6/40
Church Fenton 6/40 – 9/40
Castle Camps 9/40 – 11/40
To Egypt 11/40
North Africa 1/41 – 3/43

Above: **A ragged formation of No. 73 Squadron Hurricane Mk.Is over France in early 1940. The squadron codes were removed with both squadrons of 67 Wing AASF. (Crown)**

Right: **Early Hurricane I of No. 73 Squadron 'S for Sugar' being landed by Sergeant P V Ayerst on a basic airfield in Northern France. The full red, white and blue fin flash on the rudder was said to be for the benefit of the French fighters, although few were seen in the air. (Crown)**

Below: **'Bill' Kain of No. 73 Squadron gives the thumbs up as erks 'Gooney' Slater (left) and Dave Dalziel 'wind it up'.**

Newell 'Fanny' Orton

Joined No. 73 Squadron in 1937 and was a Flying Officer when they went to France. He had shot down five aircraft by 10 May and was awared the DFC. On 15 May he baled out of his blazing Hurricane and landed in a tree where French troops shot at him, injuring him further. After recovering and a spell at 59 OTU he was posted to No. 242 Squadron promoted to Squadron Leader and then given command of No. 54 Squadron. On 17 September 1941 he was shot down in a Spitfire and killed. He is credited with 17 aircraft destroyed, eight probables and four damaged.

Edgar 'Cobber' Kain

The New Zealander joined No. 73 Squadron in 1936. By March 1940 he had shot down five aircraft and became the RAF's first 'Ace' of the war. His aircraft was damaged by French fire twice and the Luftwaffe caused him to crash land twice more. He baled out of a Hurricane on 26 March 1940 after a combat with Me109s.

By 6 June 1940 he was the last of the original squadron still on operations and took off to return to England. He performed a slow roll over the airfield, but hit the ground and died in the wreck. He is credited with 16 aircraft destroyed and one damaged.

Right: **A posed photo dated March 1940 showing some of No. 73 Squadron's pilots. They are, left to right, Ian Scoular (in hat), 'Tommy' Tucker, Ken Campbell (rear), Graham Paul (sitting), 'Bill' Kain (with scarf), J G Perry (in coat) Reg Lovett, 'Cobber' Kain, 'Titch' Pyne, Roy Marchand.**

Flight Lieutenant R E Lovett shot down a French Potez by mistake, crash landed a burning Hurricane on 10 May 1940 and was shot down and baled out on 5 September. He had destroyed 3 aircraft before he was shot down and killed on 7 September 1940.

Below: **Hurricane I of 73 Squadron at Bu Amud in North Africa around April/May 1941, with tropical filter under the nose.**

79 SQUADRON

Code Letters:
AL & NV

Usage:
Mk.I
Nov 38 to July 41
Mk.IIb
June 41 to Dec 41
Mk.IIc
June 42 to Sept 44

Bases:
Biggin Hill 3/37 – 11/39
Manston 11/39 – 5/40
Northern France 5/40
Biggin Hill 5/40
Digby 5/40 – 6/40
Biggin Hill 6/40 – 7/40
Hawkinge 7/40
Sealand 7/40
Acklington 7/40 – 8/40
Biggin Hill 8/40 – 9/40
Pembrey 9/40 – 6/41
Fairwood Common
6/41 – 12/41
Baginton 12/41 – 3/42
To India 3/42 – 5/42
Bombay 6/42 – 12/45

Above: **A flight of three Hurricane IIbs of No. 79 Squadron during operations from Fairwood Common in late 1941. The squadron replaced Gauntlets with Hurricanes in November 1938 its first victory was a Do17 shot down on 21 November 1939. The personnel sailed to India in March 1942 and in May 1944, re-equipped with Thunderbolts. (Crown)**

Below: **The pilot readies the cockpit while the ground crew plug in the trolley-ack for starting a No. 79 Squadron Hurricane I at Biggin Hill during training before the start of WW2. (Crown)**

Below: **With the Merlin engine running and the trolley-ack unplugged the pilot climbs aboard, assisted by the ground crew, ready for another training sortie. Note the pre-war AL fuselage code. (Crown)**

81 SQUADRON

Code Letters:
53

Usage:
Mk.IIb
July 41 to Nov 41

Bases:
Debden 7/41
Leconfield 7/41 – 8/41
To Russia 8/41 – 9/41
Vaenga 9/41 – 11/41
Return to UK 11/41 – 12/41

Above: **No. 81 Squadron, shortly after its arrival in Russia, judging by the lack of snow.**

No. 81 Squadron reformed as a fighter squadron at Debden on 29 July 1941 out of 'A' Flight 504 Squadron. It became part of 151 Wing with 134 Squadron. The Wing was based at Vaenga in Russia and provided defence against German air attacks on the unloading Allied convoys until 20 November.

The squadron pilots then trained and converted Russian pilots on to the Hurricanes. The RAF crews departed for Britain on 29 November 1941, leaving the Hurricanes with the Russians. On return to Turnhouse, the squadron was equipped with Spitfires.

Above right: **The most effective means of surface transport at Vaenga was horse drawn sleighs. Here a 151 Wing Hurricane, fitted with a tropical air filter, taxies out for another sortie. (Flight)**

Right: **A No. 81 Squadron Hurricane IIb at Vaenga runs up against the wheel chocks. Aircraft and men had to operate in the very cold conditions. Note the spiral picket anchors used to tie down the Hurricanes. (Flight)**

85 SQUADRON

Code Letters:
NO & VY

Usage:
Mk.I
Sept 38 to Apr 41

Bases:
Debden 6/40 – 10/38
Aldergrove 10/41 – 11/38
Debden 11/38 – 9/39
France 9/39 – 5/40
Debden 5/40 – 6/40
Martlesham Heath 6/40 – 8/40
Debden 8/40
Croydon 8/40 – 9/40
Castle Camps 9/40
Church Fenton 9/40 – 10/40
Kirton-in-Lindsey 10/40 – 11/40
Gravesend 11/40 – 1/41
Debden 1/41 – 5/41

Above: **Armourers prepare the .303 belts for a No. 85 Squadron Hurricane in May 1940.**

Left: **HRH King George VI visited Lille-Seclin Aerodrome on 6 December 1939. Here three Hurricanes of No. 85 Squadron line up with three more of No. 87 Squadron at the end of the line. A Blenheim and pair of Gladiators are lined up opposite.**
The squadron hexagon is prominent on the fin of VY-X, a symbol adopted by the unit in WW I.

Flight Lieutenant Richard H A Lee DSO, DFC
Charterhouse educated 'Dickie' Lee joined No. 85 Squadron in 1938. He claimed the squadron's first enemy aircraft of WWII when he brought down an He111 in the Channel off Cap Gris Nez. On 11 May 1940 he was shot down and captured, but escaped and joined No. 56 Squadron. On 31 May he was shot down and rescued from the sea off Dunkirk, then rejoined No. 85 Squadron. He was last seen chasing two Ju88s on 18 August and never returned. He is believed to have had nine victories.

Flying Officer A G Lewis DFC
South African Albert Lewis went to France to join No. 85 Squadron and ran up a huge number of victories in the first few days of the invasion. On 19 May he claimed five Me109s before he was shot down. During the Battle of Britain he flew with No. 249 Squadron. In 1941 he went to Ceylon and was shot down by Zeros, but survived. By the war's end he had claimed eighteen aircraft destroyed.

On the left 'Dickie' Lee and right Albert Lewis DFC.

Above: **Squadron Leader Peter Townsend leads a No. 85 Squadron patrol in late 1940 with the Battle of Britain almost over.**

Above: **A group of No. 85 Squadron pilots. They are, from left to right, Hemingway, Howitt, Marshall and Carnaby. Kneeling with his dog is Peter Townsend, the Squadron Leader. Townsend was posted to the squadron from No. 43 Squadron on 23 May 1940. Flying Officer William Carnaby flew Defiants with No. 264 Squadron and joined No. 85 in September 1940 when it converted to night flying. He was killed on 5 February 1943 when with No. 25 Squadron.**

Above: **Yorkshire born Geoffrey 'Sammy' Allard was a Halton Apprentice and joined No. 85 Squadron in 1938. He is credited with ten victories in seven days during the Battle of France and a total of at least 19 victories. The squadron became a specialist night fighter unit and in early 1941 began to convert to Havocs. On 13 March 1941 Allard took off, but a panel came loose and the aircraft crashed. Allard and two others were killed.**

NIGHT FIGHTERS

Right: **Pilots in night vision goggles prepare for a night patrol on 11 January 1941. Left to right they are, Carnaby, Marshall, Townsend and Howitt. Peter Townsend, the CO, gained the first night victory when he shot down a Do.17Z on 25 February 1941.**

Below: **An all black Hurricane with the squadron badge.**

87 SQUADRON

Code Letters:
PD & LK

Usage:
Mk.I
July 38 to Sept 42
Mk.IIc
June 41 - Mar 44

Bases:
Debden 6/37 – 9/39
France 9/39 – 5/40
Debden 5/40
Church Fenton 5/40 – 11/40
Colerne 11/40 – 12/40
Charmy Down 12/40 – 8/41
Colerne 8/41 – 1/42
Charmy Down 1/42 – 11/42
To North Africa 11/42 – 12/42
Italy 5/43 – 9/45

Above: **No. 87 Squadron pilots scramble at a French airfield in March 1940, with the nearest pilot, Squadron Leader Dewar. All but one Hurricane still has the Watts two-blade prop.**

Above: **Hurricane Is of No. 87 Squadron at Lille-Seclin in March 1940 during a practice gas attack.**

Below: **Squadron Leader W E Coope, the CO of 87 Squadron, made an emergency landing in Belgium on 4 November 1939, becoming the first allied aircraft to be interned. (AELR Brussels)**

Below: **L2047, LK-H, damaged after an eventful landing at a basic French airfield. The aircraft was repaired and subsequently flew with several other squadrons before being written off on 25 October 1940 at Digby with 151 Squadron.**

Above: The all black Hurricane night fighter IIc BE500 LK-A of No. 87 Squadron flown by Squadron Leader Denis Smallwood DFC, who became CO in November 1941.

Ian 'Widge' Gleed

Londoner Ian Gleed, gained the nickname 'Widge' because of his slight build. He learned to fly privately and joined the RAF in 1936, joining No. 266 flying Spitfires. He was lucky to survive an accident when a Spitfire broke up in the air and after recovering from his injuries he was posted to No. 87 Squadron in France as 'A' Flight Commander in May 1940. He flew throughout the Battle of Britain and took over as Commanding Officer in December 1940. In November 1941 he was promoted to Wing Commander and lead the Middle Wallop and Ibsley Wing. In 1942 he became Wing Commander Tactics at Fighter Command HQ. He was posted to the Middle East HQ in 1943 and took over as Wing Leader of 244 Wing flying Spitfires. He was shot down on 16 April 1943 during a patrol over Cap Bon, Tunisia and killed. He wrote the book *Arise to Conquer*, published in 1942.

Gleed is credited with 13 aircraft destroyed, 7 probables, 4 damaged, 1 destroyed and one damaged on the ground.

Right: **Hurricane IIc HL864 LK-? of No. 87 Squadron fitted with long range underwing fuel tanks and with the pilot, Pilot Officer F W Mitchell ready to board. This aircraft was named *Nightingale*, a presentation Hurricane with nursing associations, and is seen at Charmy Down in September 1942.**

THE BATTLE of FRANCE

Above: **With the evacuation of the remains of the BEF from Dunkirk in June 1940, air cover was provided by a number of Hurricane squadrons based in Southern England. A number were lost during this campaign and ended up wrecked on the beach, the lucky pilots returning to Britain on board the flotilla of small boats.**

Following the declaration of War against Germany on 1 September 1939, as part of an established agreement, the British Expedition ary Force (BEF) was sent across the Channel to take up positions along the Franco-Belgian border. The contribution by the RAF was the air component of the BEF and the Advanced Air Striking Force (AASF). The former was tasked with the support and protection of the BEF and included Nos. 85 and 87 Squadrons equipped with Hurricanes. In addition to the light bomber units with the AASF, Nos. 1 and 73 Squadrons formed 67 Wing, equipped with Hurricanes and were tasked with air defence over the British occupied areas of Northern France as well as providing escort to the vulnerable Blenheim and Battle bombers.

The Hurricane units in France were initially still equipped with early Mk.Is fitted with Merlin IIs driving fixed pitch Watts wooden propellers and the priority was to re-equip with newer models. There was also pressure from the French for more squadrons to be sent to France, but this was resisted by Air Chief Marshal Dowding, Commander in Chief of Fighter Command, who was concerned about sending more pilots and fighters to what he believed was a lost cause.

The first RAF victory in France was credited to Flight Lieutenant P P Hanks of No. 1 Squadron on 30 October 1939, a total of 26 victories were claimed by the squadron during the Battle of France. By May 1940, No. 73 Squadron had claimed 30 victories with Flying Officer E J "Cobber" Kain being awarded the DFC for becoming the first "ace" of the war with five enemy aircraft destroyed.

Both Nos. 607 and 615 Squadrons were also posted to France equipped with Gladiators, 607 Squadron replacing them with Hurricanes in April 1939 soon followed by 615 Squadron. There was no co-ordination of the fighter defensive operations, the squadrons operating independently from very rudimentary airfields which were poorly defended. The German offensive began on 10 May 1939 with air and ground attacks on neutral Holland in a rapid advance which included Belgium on 13 May where their force of Hurricanes was soon destroyed.

By 15 May Holland had been occupied, the Belgian Air Force had ceased to exist and losses of British aircraft from Bf109s, including Hurricanes was growing. The squadrons of the AASF had to fall back to the south to avoid being over-run, the Hurricanes mainly being used to defend their own airfields. Hurricanes were flown to France as reinforcements and a number of squadrons were deployed to France each day to help support the units already there.

On 17 May the German advances separated the Allied Northern and Southern Armies and as the advances progressed, the AASF units continued to evacuate their airfields and began to withdraw south, leaving behind any unserviceable aircraft which were destroyed before departure. Hurricane pilots with the BEF claimed 57 victories with 20 probables, although the figure was closer to 39 German aircraft destroyed. With the Hurricanes being totally outnumbered at least 33 were destroyed or crash landed with seven pilots killed and five taken prisoner. Hurricanes with the AASF claimed 74 victories with 25 probables, although German recorded around 47 aircraft. The AASF lost 22 Hurricanes shot down and 13 damaged with eight pilots killed and three taken prisoner.

On 20 May the German advances reached the coast and the BEF units evacuated back to Britain, with the AASF squadrons remaining in France. A total of 452 Hurricanes had been sent to France, but only 66 returned to Britain. Of the 386 aircraft lost, 178 were abandoned as unserviceable and destroyed by the retreating Allied forces. During the 11 days of Battle leading to the evacuation of Dunkirk the Air Component lost 203 Hurricanes, of which about a half were in combat. A total of 56 RAF and FAA pilots had been killed with a further 18 taken prisoner. Hurricane pilots claimed some 499 victories and 123 probables, although German records suggest 299 losses with 65 seriously damaged. The three AASF units, Nos. 1, 73 and 501 Squadrons remained in France moving south until being withdrawn via the Channel Islands on 19 June. During the Battle of France over 200 pilots were lost, including 29 squadron and flight commanders.

Above: **A No. 85 Squadron Hurricane, part of the BEF in France, ready to go from Lille. Together with No. 87 Squadron it suffered particularly heavy casualties in the first days.**

Above: **A perfect target. The Belgian Air Force lost eleven Hurricanes after the enemy attacked on May 10 1940. (Air Museum, Brussels)**

Above: **No. 85 Squadron during a practice air attack.**

Above: **A bent No. 87 Squadron machine.**

Below: **With the rapid German advances most of the Belgian Hurricanes were destroyed or damaged on the first day of the invasion as they were lined up unprotected on Schaffen-Diest airfield. (Air Museum, Brussels)**

Above: **Despite the heroic efforts of the Hurricane pilots and the French fighter pilots the Luftwaffe quickly established itself in France. Here the Do17 equipped 4./KG77 makes use of grass airfield.**

Left: **The carnage of defeat in France as captured in a snap taken by a Luftwaffe airman. The roads leading to Dunkirk were littered with abandoned vehicles and dead animals as the BEF struggled to escape.**

Left: **Another souvenir photograph shows a burnt out Hurricane slowly sinking into the sand of a French beach. 452 Hurricanes had been sent to France, but only 66 returned to Britain. As Dowding observed, had further aircraft been committed to the defence of France, the defence of Britain would have been seriously jeopardized.**

96 SQUADRON

Code Letters:
ZJ

Usage:
Mk.I
Oct 40 to May 41
Mk. IIc
Sept 41 to Jan 42

Bases:
Cranage 12/40 – 10/41
Wrexham 10/41 – 10/42

Above: **One of No. 96 Squadron's black Hurricanes in February 1941, just before the arrival at the squadron of its first Defiant. (Z Hurt)**

Right: **Hurricane I night fighter P3712 ZJ-J of No. 96 Squadron at Cranage. The squadron reformed on 18 December 1940 from 422 Flight for the night defence of the Liverpool area, scoring a victory against an He 111 on 12 March 1941, shortly before converting to Defiants.**

Below: **No. 98 Squadron was equipped with Battles and acquired Hurricanes in June 1941 to defend the Allied Fleet at the Icelandic end of the Russian convoys. It was disbanded in July 1941, the Hurricane element becoming No. 1423 Flight.**

98 SQUADRON

Code Letters:
None

Usage:
Mk.IIa
June 41 to July 41

Base:
Kaldadarnes, Iceland
6/41 - 7/41

111 SQUADRON

Code Letters:

TM & JU

Usage:

Mk.I
Dec 37 to Apr 41

Bases:

Northolt 7/34 – 10/39
Acklington 10/39 – 12/39
Drem 12/39 – 2/40
Wick 2/40 – 5/40
Northolt 5/40
Digby 5/40
North Weald 5/40 – 6/40
Croydon 6/40 – 8/40
Debden 8/40 – 9/40
Croydon 9/40
Drem 9/40 – 10/40
Dyce 10/40 – 7/41

Above: **No. 111 Squadron introduced the Hurricane into RAF service, with deliveries commencing in December 1937. As a demonstration of the new aircraft's performance the CO, Squadron Leader John Gillan, flew from Edinburgh to Northolt (400 miles) in a record time of 48 minutes on 10 February 1938 with the benefit of a tail-wind.**

Below: **MPs visit the squadron on 27 April 1938. The pilot in the white overalls is Sergeant J T Craig who is credited with at least five victories during the Battle of Britain. He was shot down and baled out on 31 August 1940 and was posted to No. 56 OTU as an instructor. During a training flight over Norfolk on 2 June 1941 he was in collision with another Hurricane and died in the resulting crash.**

Above: **No. 111 Squadron was based at Wick in February 1940 for the air defence of the Allied fleet at Scapa Flow. Hurricane I L2001 JU-B was lost at Hatfield on 19 June 1940, when Sergeant Pascoe was killed in a take-off crash.**

Pilot Officer R J W Brown

Ronald Brown joined the RAF as a Halton Apprentice in 1929 and trained as an engine fitter. He played football at Cranwell where his ability earned him a posting to No. 10 (Bomber) Squadron who wanted his sporting skills more than his technical ability. He learned to fly in 1936 and joined No. 111 Squadron in 1937.

During the Battle of France the squadron operated from Northolt, flying daily to France. Flying an escort to Blenheims on June 6 1940 he was shot down near Abbeville by an Me109 and baled out with injuries. He found a retreating army unit who saw him safely to a field hospital and from there he was evacuated. He flew his next patrol with the squadron on 15 August and flew throughout the Battle of Britain before being posted to No. 260 Squadron in a training capacity in December 1940.

Brown then left operational flying and spent a time at the Air Fighting Development Unit at Duxford before moving on to the Ministry of Aircraft Production where he was involved with testing and development. He retired from the RAF in 1947 as a Wing Commander to follow a career in sales and marketing for Percival, BAC and British Aerospace.

Below: **Sergeant O Hruby, a Czech with No. 111 Squadron, at Dyce in early 1941 before re-equipping with Spitfires. (Z Hurt)**

116 SQUADRON

Code Letters:
II

Usage:
Mk.I & IIa
Nov 41 to May 45

Bases:
Hendon 4/41 – 4/42
Heston 4/42 – 12/43
Croydon 12/43 – 7/44
North Weald 7/44 – 8/44
Gatwick 8/44 – 9/44
Redhill 9/44 – 5/45
Hornchurch 5/45

Above: **Formed at Hatfield on 17 February 1941, No. 116 Squadron was the first calibration unit. Its main duty was the calibration of AA gun direction radars using a variety of aircraft, including Hurricanes. The squadron disbanded on 26 May 1945.**

Above: **No. 121 Squadron pilots in November 1941. The squadron was formed at Kirton-in-Lindsey on 14 May 1941 as the second of the three American volunteer pilot *Eagle* squadrons and part of 12 Group. After equipping with Spitfires, the squadron transferred to the USAAF as 335 (Pursuit) Squadron at Debden on 29 September 1942.**

121 (EAGLE) SQUADRON

Code Letters:
AV

Usage:
Mk.I
May 41 to July 41
Mk.IIb
July 41 to Nov 41

Base:
Kirton-in-Lindsey 5/41 - 12/41

Below: **Formed at Coltishall as the third and final *Eagle* squadron, No. 133 Squadron, became operational flying East Coast convoy patrols. Here the squadron shows off after converting to Spitfires at Fowlmere in October 1941.**

133 (EAGLE) SQUADRON

Code Letters:
MD

Usage:
Mk.IIb
Aug 41 to Dec 41

Bases:
Coltishall 7/40 – 8/41
Duxford 8/41 – 9/41
Colly Weston 9/41 – 10/41
Fowlmere 10/41

134 SQUADRON

Code Letters:
G & GQ

Usage:
Mk.IIb
July 41 to Oct 41
Dec 41 to Feb 42
Mk.IIc
Mar 43 to Apr 43
Nov 43 to Aug 44

Bases:
Leconfield 7/41 – 8/41
Vaenga 9/41 – 11/41
Catterick 12/41 – 1/42
Eglinton 1/41 – 3/42
Baginton 3/42 – 4/42
To Egypt 4/42 – 6/42
Palestine 11/43
India 11/43 – 7/45

Above: **Three Hurricanes of No. 134 Squadron overfly Z3768 of No. 81 Squadron at readiness on the ground at Vaenga in September 1941 during deployment to Russia.**

Squadron Leader A G Miller (left) No. 134 Squadron

Anthony Miller started the war with No. 600 Squadron before a spell at 11 Group HQ and the FIU. He commanded No. 17 Squadron from August 1940 to July 1941, when he left to form 134 Squadron. On his return from Russia he went back to the FIU and was then posted to No. 600 Squadron again, this time as its CO. He retired from the RAF in 1946.

Squadron Leader M Rook (right) No. 81 Squadron

Michael Rook joined No.504 Squadron in 1938, fought with it in France and the Battle of Britain and took command in March 1941. He left the squadron in July 1941 to form No. 81 Squadron. On return from Russia he assumed command of No. 43 Squadron and took it North Africa. Rook retired from the RAF in 1946, but was killed in a flying accident in 1948.

Right: **Hurricane 'GO' of No. 134 Squadron. The squadron used the letter 'G' followed by the individual aircraft letter during its time in Russia. The squadron embarked on *HMS Argus* for Russia as part of 151 Wing at Vaenga. During a German raid on 6 October 1941 No. 134 Squadron destroyed two Ju88s, and soon after the squadron began to train Soviet pilots to fly the Hurricanes. On 28 October all aircraft were handed over to the Russian Air Force and the personnel of No. 134 Squadron returned to Britain.**

137 SQUADRON

Code Letters:

SF

Usage:

Mk.IV
June 43 to Jan 44

Bases:

Rochford 6/43 – 8/43
Manston 8/43 – 1/44

Above: **No. 137 Squadron operated RP and cannon armed Hurricane Mk.IVs on ground attack duties until replaced by Typhoons from January 1944 at Manston. Hurricane BP173 was originally built as a Mk.IIb, but was seventh conversion to a Mk.IV similar to those flown by 137 Squadron. It was used for RP trials at A&AEE in July 1942.**

Left: **BP173 was used for testing rocket and cannon equipped ground attack Hurricanes. No. 137 Squadron replaced its Whirlwinds in June 1943 and first used them on operations over Holland on 2 September 1943. After six months of Hurricane operations, the replacement Typhoons arrived, with the first operation by the new type taking place on 8 February 1944.**

Below: **P3221 SO-K at Westhampnett in July 1940. In March 1940 No. 145 Squadron began replacing Blenheims with Hurricanes at Croydon and in May provided support for the squadrons in France. Following a rest period at Drem, the squadron returned to 11 Group and began converting to Spitfires.**

145 SQUADRON

Code Letters:

SO

Usage:

Mk.I
Mar 40 to Feb 41

Bases:

Croydon 10/39 – 5/40
Filton 5/40
Tangmere 5/40 – 7/40
Westhampnett 7/40 – 8/40
Drem 8/40 – 10/40
Tangmere 10/40 – 5/41

151 SQUADRON

Code Letters:
GG & DZ

Usage:
Mk.I
Dec 38 to June 41
Mk.IIc
Apr 41 to Jan 42

Bases:
North Weald 8/36 – 8/40
Martlesham Heath 5/40 – 8/40
Stapleford 8/40 – 9/40
Digby 9/40 – 11/40
Bramcote 11/40 – 12/40
Wittering 12/40 – 4/43

Above: **L1768 showing the pre-war 'GG' codes. After this incident the aircraft was repaired and went on to serve with No. 87 Squadron, before going to a series of OTUs and non operational units. It was not struck off charge until September 1944.**

Wing Commander F V Beamish

Irish born Victor Beamish was invalided out of the RAF in 1933 with tuberculosis. He re-joined in 1937, becoming the commander of North Weald, a post he held throughout the Battle of Britain. During that time he flew in combat with No. 151 Squadron and others based on 'his' airfield. On 28 March 1942 he was leading the North Weald Wing over the Channel when he was shot down by an Me109 and crashed into the sea. His body was never found.

Flight Lieutenant R P Stevens

Richard Playne Stevens had been a pre-war airline pilot. His night flying experience served him well when No. 151 Squadron turned to night fighting at which he excelled. Even though the Hurricane could not carry radar, he destroyed 14 aircraft - all at night. He joined No. 253 Squadron in November 1941 to begin night intruder operations. It was on one of these sorties that he crashed and was killed near Gilze-Rijen on 15 December 1941.

Right: **Night fighting Hurricane IIc V6931 DZ-D of No. 151 Squadron at Wittering in 1941 with black finish. In December 1938 the squadron replaced its Gauntlets with Hurricanes. It provided support in France using Vitry as an advanced landing ground. No. 151 Squadron took part in the Battle of Britain, but on 1 September moved to 12 Group for a rest. In November the squadron was allocated to night fighting and the Hurricanes were supplemented by Defiants which it kept until the more capable Mosquito night fighters came in April 1942.**

Above: **Forerunner to the Typhoon, Hurricane Mk.IV KZ706, fitted with 'Long Tom' rocket rails for tests.**

164 SQUADRON 2nd TAF

Code Letters: FJ

Usage: Mk.IV Feb 43 to Feb 44

Bases:

Middle Wallop 2/43 – 6/43
Warmwell 6/43 – 8/43
Manston 8/43 – 9/43
Fairlop 9/43 – 3/44

174 SQUADRON 2nd TAF

Code Letters: XP

Usage: Mk.IIb Mar 42 to Apr 43

Bases:

Manston 3/42 – 7/42
Fowlmere 7/42
Manston 7/42 – 9/42
Warmwell 9/42
Manston 9/42 – 1242
Odiham 12/42 – 3/43
Chilbolton 3/43
Grove 3/43
Odiham 3/43 – 4/43

175 SQUADRON 2nd TAF

Code Letters: HH

Usage: Mk.IIb Mar 42 to Apr 43

Bases:

Warmwell 3/42 – 10/42
Harrowbeer 10/42 – 12/42
Gatwick 12/42 – 1/43
Odiham 1/43 – 3/43
Stoney Cross 3/43 – 4/43

181 SQUADRON 2nd TAF

Code Letters: EL

Usage: Mk.I Sept 42 to Dec 42

Bases:

Duxford 9/42 – 12/42
Snailwell 12/42 – 3/43
Cranfield 3/43
Snailwell 3/43 – 4/43
Lasham 4/43 – 6/43

164 Squadron, 2nd TAF
Service history: Swapped its Spitfires for Hurricanes in February 1943 and began attacks on shipping in June. The Hurricanes were replaced by Typhoons in February 1944.
174(Mauritius) Squadron, 2nd TAF
Service history: Formed at Manston on 3 March 1942 with many No. 607 Squadron personnel. The squadron was allocated to fighter-bomber duties with the first raid on 28 March at Berck-sur-mer. The Hurricanes were replaced by Typhoons from April 1943.
175 Squadron, 2nd TAF
Service history: Formed at Warmwell as a fighter-bomber squadron on 3 March 1942 with Hurricanes. Operations were mainly against shipping and in April 1943 the Hurricanes were replaced by Typhoons.
181 Squadron, 2nd TAF
Service history: Formed at Duxford on 1 September 1942 with Hurricane Is and Typhoons, as there were still teething troubles with the Typhoons. The squadron was operational at the end of November and as experience was gained with Typhoons, the Hurricanes were phased out.
182 Squadron, 2nd TAF
Service history: Formed at Martlesham Heath on 1 September with a mix of Hurricanes and Typhoons with the first operation on 3 January 1943. The Hurricanes were progressively withdrawn as the Typhoons were delivered.
183 Squadron, 2nd TAF
Service history: Formed at Church Fenton on 1 November 1942 with Typhoon Ias and a few Hurricanes, 183 Squadron started operational training in March 1943 with the first operation in April.
184 Squadron, 2nd TAF
Service history: Formed at Colerne on 1 December 1942 for anti-tank operations with Hurricane IIds. Soon after the squadron changed to anti-shipping operations with rockets. Attacks were mounted against Noball targets from December 1943, but Typhoons appeared from December, until the last Hurricane operation in March 1944.
186 Squadron, Army Support
Service history: Formed at Drem on 17 April 1943 and received the first Hurricanes at Ayr in August armed with 40mm cannons and rockets for Army support. The squadron converted to Typhoons in late November.

Above: **Line up of No. 174 *Mauritius* Squadron Hurricane IIbs at Manston in May 1942.**

Above: **No. 175 Squadron showing the 'HH' code and a bomb trolley in the foreground.**

182 SQUADRON 2nd TAF

Code Letters:
XM

Usage:
Mk.I
Sept 42 to Dec 42

Bases:
Martlesham Heath 9/42 – 12/42
Sawbridgeworth 12/42 – 1/43
Martlesham Heath 1/43 – 3/43
Middle Wallop 3/43 – 4/43

183 SQUADRON 2nd TAF

Code Letters:
HF

Usage:
Mk.I
Nov 42 to Feb 43

Base:
Church Fenton 11/42 – 3/43

184 SQUADRON 2nd TAF

Code Letters:
BR

Usage:
Mk.IId
Dec 42 to May 43
Mk.IV
May 43 to Mar 44

Bases:
Colerne 12/42 – 343
Chilbolton 3/43
Eastchurch 3/43 – 5/43
Merston 5/43 – 6/43
Manston 6/43 – 8/43
122 & 125 A/F 8/43 – 10/43
Detling 10/43 – 3/44

186 SQUADRON Army Support

Code Letters:
AP

Usage:
Mk.IV
Aug 43 to Nov 43

Base:
Ayr 8/43 - 1/44

213 SQUADRON

Code Letters:
AK

Usage:
Mk.I
Jan 39 to Mar 42
Mk.IIc
Jan 42 to May 44

Bases:
Wittering 5/38 – 5/40
Merville 5/40
Wittering 5/40
Biggin Hill 5/40 – 6/40
Wittering 6/40
Biggin Hill 6/40
Exeter 6/40 – 9/40
Tangmere 9/40 – 11/40
Leconfield 11/40 – 1/41
Driffield 1/41 – 2/41
Castletown 2/41 – 5/41
HMS Furious 5/41
To Egypt and North Africa

Above: **Hurricane I of No. 213 Squadron being re-armed at Biggin Hill on 3 June 1940. The squadron had converted to Hurricanes from Gauntlets in January 1939 at Wittering, from where convoy patrols were flown. Following some action in France the squadron took part in the Battle of Britain, not retiring for rest until November when it went north again for coastal patrols.**

Left: **A Hurricane I of No. 229 Squadron being refuelled and turned round during the Battle of Britain with the ground crew wearing protective helmets and keeping a watch for enemy raiders. The guns have been fired recently as the fabric patches have been blown off.**

229 SQUADRON

Code Letters:
RE & HB

Usage:
Mk.I
Mar 40 to May 41
Mk.IIc
Sept 41 to Apr 42

Bases:
Digby 10/39 – 6/40
Wittering 6/40 – 9/40
Northolt 9/40 – 12/40
Wittering 12/40
Speke 12/40 – 5/41
To Egypt and North Africa

Above: **Dated April 1941, this obviously posed photo shows an unusually large number of armourers in no hurry to re-arm a Hurricane, on a particularly muddy airfield.**

232 SQUADRON

Code Letters:
EF

Usage:
Mk.I
July 40 to Nov 41
Mk.IIb
Aug 41 to Feb 42

Bases:
Sumburgh 7/40
Castletown 7/40 – 10/40
Skitten 10/40
Drem 10/40 – 11/40
Skitten 11/40 – 12/40
Elgin 12/40 – 4/41
Montrose 4/41 – 7/41
Abbotsinch 7/41
Ouston 7/41 – 11/41
To Singapore 11/41 – 1/42
Seletar 1/42 – 2/42

Pilot Officer R F T Doe

Bob Doe trained with the RAFVR and joined No. 234 Squadron in November 1939 flying Spitfires. He proved to be a very successful fighter pilot and shot down twelve aircraft during the Battle of Britain. In September 1940 his squadron was posted to Cornwall to recover, but Doe was posted to No. 238 Squadron and had to change from flying Spitfires to Hurricanes. On 10 October 1940 he was shot down over Dorset and baled out injured in both leg and shoulder.
He rejoined the squadron in December, but a few weeks later, on 3 January 1941, he crash landed a Hurricane at night after engine failure. The crash was severe and although he survived he suffered serious facial injuries which required 22 plastic surgery operations to re-build, yet he returned to flying in May 1941. He retired from the RAF in 1966.

238 SQUADRON

Code Letters:
VK & KC

Usage:
Mk.I
June 40 to Mar 41
Mk.IIa
Mar 41 - May 41
Mk.IIb
May 42 - Oct 42
Mk.IIc
Sept 41 to Feb 42
Oct 42 - Sept 43

Bases:
Tangmere 5/40 – 6/40
Middle Wallop 6/40 – 8/40
St Eval 8/40 – 9/40
Middle Wallop 9/40
Chilbolton 9/40 – 1/41
Middle Wallop 1/41 – 2/41
Chilbolton 2/41 – 4/41
Pembrey 4/41
Chilbolton 4/41 – 5/41

239 SQUADRON

Code Letters:
HB

Usage:
Mk.I & IIc
Jan 42 to May 42

Bases:
Gatwick 2/41 - 8/42

Below: **The code letters 'KC' on a No. 238 Squadron Hurricane after the move to North Africa.**

242 SQUADRON

Code Letters:

LE

Usage:

Mk.I
Feb 40 to Apr 41
Mk.IIb
Feb 41 to Mar 42

Bases:

Church Fenton 10/39 – 5/40
Biggin Hill 5/40
France 5/40 – 6/40
Coltishall 6/40 – 8/40
Duxford 8/40 – 12/40
Martlesham Heath 12/40 – 4/41
Stapleford 4/41 – 5/41
North Weald 5/41 – 7/41
Manston 7/41 – 9/41
Valley 9/41 – 12/41
To Asia 12/41

Above: **Led by Squadron Leader Douglas Bader, No. 242 Squadron climbs away from Duxford in October 1940 to form up with the Duxford Wing. The squadron became operational on 23 March 1940 at Church Fenton with mainly Canadian aircrew who had joined the RAF before the war. It saw its first action over France and covered the withdrawal of the BEF. The squadron re-equipped at Coltishall and was again operational on 9 July for the Battle of Britain. Douglas Bader became the CO in June 1940 and with the move to Duxford in August, instigated the 'Big Wing' attacks from 12 Group in support of 11 Group in the Battle of Britain. In early 1941 the squadron was involved in ground attack and convoy patrols, but losses were heavy. The squadron embarked for Singapore in December 1941, but it succumbed to Japanese attacks and ceased to exist in Java around 10 March 1942.**

Flight Lieutenant William Lidstone McKnight

Canadian 'Willie' McKnight was born in 1918 and was studying medicine at the University of Alberta when he joined the RAF in February 1939. In November 1939 he joined the mainly Canadian No. 242 Squadron, but gained his first victory with No. 615 Squadron in France. Back with 242 he fought over Dunkirk and covered the retreat through France south to the Biscay ports until mid June.

Back in England at the end of August he continued his highly successful combat career and brought down six more aircraft to bring his total of aircraft destroyed to 17, with five others shared or probable. On 12 January 1941, with the rank of Flying Officer, he took part in one of the early 'Rhubarb' operations to France and vanished after strafing ground troops, presumably becoming a victim to patrolling Me109s.

Squadron Leader Douglas Robert Stewart Bader

Perhaps the best known fighter pilot in the RAF, Douglas Bader famously lost his legs after a flying accident in December 1931. Prior to that he had been a sportsman and aerobatic pilot.

He was invalided out of the service, but was accepted back in November 1939 and flew with Nos. 19 and 222 Squadrons before being given command of 242. He led the 'Big Wing' and championed the tactic. In March 1941 he became Wing Commander Flying at Tangmere, one of the first Wing Leaders. He is believed to have been shot down, or collided with another aircraft, over France on 9 August 1941, baled out and was taken prisoner. Down but not beaten he made several escape attempts and finished the war in Colditz. Post war he was much decorated and an encouragement to many limbless people until his death from a heart attack in 1982.

Flight Lieutenant George Eric Ball

Kent born Ball joined No. 19 Squadron and fought over the Dunkirk beaches before moving to 242. He was credited with six aircraft destroyed and received the DFC. In January 1941 he went to the Middle East to fly with No. 73 Squadron, but on 12 April flew into a sand storm and was forced to crash land behind the lines. He remained a prisoner until the end of the war. After the war he became CO of No. 222 Squadron, but was killed flying a Meteor on 1 February 1946 at the age of 27.

Left: **Three 'aces' of No. 242 Squadron. They are, left to right' F/Lt McKnight, S/Ldr Bader, F/Lt Ball.**

245

SQUADRON

Code Letters:

DX & MR

Usage:

Mk.I
Mar 40 to Aug 41
Mk.IIb
Aug 41 to Sept 42
Mk.IIc
May 42 to Jan 43

Bases:

Leconfield 10/39 – 5/40
Drem 5/40 – 6/40
Turnhouse 6/41 – 7/40
Aldergrove 7/40 – 6/41
Ballyhalbert 6/41 – 9/41
Chilbolton 9/41 – 12/41
Middle Wallop 12/41 – 10/42
Charmy Down 10/42 – 1/43

Above: **A loose formation of Hurricane Is of No. 245 Squadron in late 1940 operating from Aldergrove. The nearest aircraft is P3762, DX-F.**

Above: **Hurricane IIbs of No. 245 Squadron at Chilbolton in late 1941. (Z Hurt)**

Above: **Squadron Leader John Simpson who took command in November 1940 after a career with No. 43 Squadron.**

Left: **Hurricane I W9200 DX-? of No. 245 Squadron at Aldergrove. It was flown by the CO, Squadron Leader J W C Simpson in April 1941. The squadron had been formed at Leconfield on 30 October 1939 with Blenheims and later Battles. The Hurricanes came in March 1940 for the defence of northern Britain. There were squadron detachments over France in May 1940 and in April 1941 it became responsible for night defence of Belfast. The squadron flew ground attack over France and flew with Turbinlite Havocs. In January 1943 the squadron converted to Typhoons.**

247 SQUADRON

Code Letters:
HP & ZY

Usage:

Mk.I
Dec 40 to June 41
Mk.IIa
June 41 to Dec 41
Mk.IIb
Aug 41 to Dec 41
Aug 42 to Mar 43
Mk.IIc
Aug 41 to Mar 43

Bases:

Roborough 8/40 – 2/41
St Eval 2/41 – 5/41
Portreath 5/41 – 6/41
Predannack 6/41 – 5/42
Exeter 5/42 – 9/42
High Ercall 9/42 – 4/43

Above: **During 1942, No. 247 Squadron spent most of the time on night-fighter defence duties with Hurricane IIcs, BD936 ZY-S in overall matt black being an example.**

Pilot Officer Thomas Francis Neil

Tom 'Ginger' Neil shot down 12 aircraft, with others shared or damaged, while with No. 249 Squadron. On 7 November 1940 he baled out after W/Cdr Beamish chopped his tail off. He moved with the squadron to Malta, but left in December 1941. He survived the war and became a test pilot, retiring from the RAF in 1964.

Flight Lieutenant Eric J B Nicolson VC

On 16 August 1940, Nicolson lead an attack on Bf110s but was bounced from behind by Bf 109s. Nicolson's Hurricane was set alight but he continued his attack on the Bf110s before bailing out with extensive burns. Following a long stay in hospital he was awarded the Victoria Cross, the only one in Fighter Command.

Below: **No. 249 Squadron at North Weald in 1940. They are, from left to right, P/O P R F Burton, F/Lt Barton, F/Lt A G Lewis DFC, P/O Crossie, F/O T Neil, P/O J Beazley, S/Ldr J Grandy (CO), P/O G Barclay, F/Lt K Lofts.**

249 SQUADRON

Code Letters:
GN

Usage:

Mk.I
June 40 to Feb 41
Mk.IIa
Feb 41 to Apr 41
Mk.IIb
June 41 to Mar 42
Mk.IIc
June 41 to Mar 42

Bases:

Church Fenton 5/40
Leconfield 5/40 – 7/40
Church Fenton 7/40 – 8/40
Boscombe Down 8/40 – 9/40
North Weald 9/40 – 5/41
To Malta 5.41
Ta Kali 5.41 - 11.42

253 SQUADRON

Code Letters:
SW

Usage:
Mk.I
Jan 40 to Sept 41
Mk.IIb
July 41 to Sept 42
Mk.IIa
Oct 41 to Feb 42
Mk.IIc
Jan 42 to Sept 42
Nov 42 to Sept 43

Bases:
Northolt 2/40 – 5/40
Kenley 5/40
Kirton-in-Lindsey 5/40 – 7/40
Turnhouse 7/40 – 8/40
Prestwick 8/40
Kenley 8/40 – 1/41
Leconfield 1/41 – 2/41
Skeabrae 2/41 – 9/41
Hibaldstow 9/41 – 5/42
Shoreham 5/42
Hibaldstow 5/42 – 6/42
Friston 6/42 – 7/42
Hibaldstow 7/42 – 8/42
Friston 8/42
Hibaldstow 8/42 – 11/42
To North Africa 11/42

Above: **L2020, SW-A of No. 253 Squadron after a mishap. It was repaired and sent to 7 OTU.**

Squadron Leader T P Gleave

Tom Gleave was born in 1908 and learned to fly in 1929. He joined the RAF in 1930. In 1933 he attempted to be the first to fly to Ceylon, but was forced down in Turkey, and then became an instructor. When war was declared he was Fighter Command's Bomber Liaison Officer and was given command of No. 253 Squadron in June 1940. Although still with the squadron, Squadron Leader Starr was CO. On 31 August 1940 Starr was shot down and killed at 08.25 hours and Gleave assumed command, but was himself shot down at 13.02 hours. The burns he received were terrible and he became the most famous of McIndoe's plastic surgery 'Guinea Pigs'. With skin grafts to his face and limbs he returned to operations within the year and became CO of RAF Manston. He ended the war as Head of Air Plans at SHEAF.

Right: **A No. 253 Squadron Hurricane I at readiness in 1940. 253 joined in the Battle of Britain on 29 August 1940 when it was very active. Early the next year the squadron returned north on convoy patrols as well as air defence.**

Below: **B Flight of No. 253 Squadron Hurricane IIbs being prepared for night operations at Hibaldstow in December 1941. The nearest aircraft, Z3971, carries the name "Samasthans II", the second aircraft "Hyderabad City" and the third "The Paighs".**

255 SQUADRON

Code Letters:
YD

Usage:
Mk.I
Mar 41 to July 41

Bases:
Kirton-in-Lindsey 11/40 – 5/41
Hibaldstow 5/41 – 9/41

257 SQUADRON

Code Letters:
DT & FM

Usage:
Mk.I
June 40 to June 41
Mk.IIc
Apr 41 to Aug 41
Jan 42 - Sept 42
Mk.IIb
June 41 to Sept 42

Bases:
Hendon 5/40 – 7/40
Northolt 7/40 – 8/40
Debden 8/40 – 9/40
Martlesham Heath
9/40 – 10/40
North Weald 10/40 – 12/40
Coltishall 12/40 – 11/41
Honiley 11/41 – 6/42
High Ercall 6/42 – 9/42

Above: **Stanford Tuck in V6864, DT-A, leads a flight of No. 257 Squadron Hurricane Is from a snow covered Coltishall in January 1941.**

Squadron Leader R S Tuck
Bob Tuck was born in 1916 in London. He began the war on Spitfires with No. 65 Squadron with which he fought over Dunkirk and during the Battle of Britain. He took command of 257 on 11 September 1940 and continued to run up his 'score'.
He was shot down over France and captured on 28 January 1942. He escaped in 1945 and fought with the Russian infantry before returning to England.

Left: **Squadron Leader R "Bob" Stanford Tuck DSO DFC* commanded No. 257 (Burma) Squadron from October 1940 until July 1941.**

Below: **The 'ER' codes were worn by No. 258 Squadron shortly before its posting overseas.**

258 SQUADRON

Code Letters:
ER & ZT

Usage:
Mk.I
Dec 40 to Apr 41
Mk.IIa
Apr 41 to Feb 42

Bases:
Acklington 12/40 – 2/41
Jurby 2/41 – 4/41
Valley 4/41
Kenley 4/41 - 6/41
Redhill 6/41
Kenley 6/41 - 7/41
Martlesham Heath 7/41 -10/41
Debden 10/40- 11/41
To the Far East

260

SQUADRON

Code Letters:

HS

Usage:

Mk.I

Dec 40 to Feb 42

Bases:

Castletown 11/40 – 12/40

Skitten 12/40 – 1/41

Castletown 1/41 – 2/41

Skitten 2/41 – 4/41

Drem 4/41 – 5/41

To Palestine 4/41 – 8/41

Left: **Ground crews of No. 260 Squadron at Skitten in December 1941.**

Above: **No. 263 Squadron briefly operated Hurricane Mk.Is from June to November 1940.**

The Rescue Squadrons

The rescue squadrons were first formed in the early part of World War 2 to fulfil an urgent need to reduce the serious losses of valuable aircrew who had abandoned their stricken aircraft, parachuted into the sea and died in the dinghies through exposure and not being located. For surface search and rescue (SAR) special launches were brought into service in larger numbers towards the end of 1940. At the same time surplus Lysanders were allocated to air search with the capability of dropping dinghies, supplies and survival equipment to downed aircrew, the main areas of operation being the south and south-east. So effective were these operations that a nationwide Air Sea Rescue Directorate was established in January 1941, resulting in a rise of ditched aircrew saved from 20 to 33 percent. As additional types of aircraft were allocated to SAR units, the Walrus amphibians became the principle rescue type with its ability to land often alongside survivors. As the SAR organisation expanded during the war to include long range aircraft, single engine fighters such as Hurricanes were used for short range searches, alerting the rescue organisation to any survivors found at sea to be picked up by amphibian or rescue boats.

263

SQUADRON

Code Letters:

HE

Usage:

Mk.I

June 40 to Nov 40

Bases:

Drem 6/40

Grangemouth 6/40 – 9/40

Drem 9/40 – 11/40

Whirlwind Squadron

Formed at Filton on 2 October 1939 with Gladiators the squadron went to Norway, but suffered heavy losses and operated with No. 46 Squadron's Hurricanes. The surviving men and machines were lost when *HMS Glorious* was sunk attempting to evacuate them to Britain.

The unit began to reform at Drem on 10 June with Hurricanes pending the arrival of Whirlwinds, the first of which arrived on 6 July and the last Hurricane left by November.

276

RESCUE SQUADRON

Code Letters:

AQ

Usage:

Mk.I

Dec 41 to Jan 42

Bases:

Harrowbear 10/41 – 4/44

279

RESCUE SQUADRON

Code Letters:

OS

Usage:

Mk.IIc & IV

April 45 to June 45

Bases:

Thornaby 10/44 - 9/45

285

AAC
SQUADRON

Code Letters:
VG

Usage:
Mk.IIc
Jan 44 to June 45

Bases:
Woodvale 8/43 – 11/44
Andover 11/44 – 1/45
North Weald 1/45 – 6/45
Weston Zoyland 6/45

286

AAC
SQUADRON

Code Letters:
NW

Usage:
Mk. I, IIc & IV
Nov 41 to May 45

Bases:
Filton 11/41 – 1/42
Colerne 9/42 – 10/42
Weston Zoyland 11/43 – 4/44
Weston Zoyland 9/44 – 5/45

Anti-aircraft Co-operation Squadrons (AAC)

Before World War 2 anti-aircraft weapons were fairly basic and any target practice was usually provided by regular operational squadrons. With the massive build up of the armed forces from 1939 there was a need to provide continuous practice for Army and Navy guns. As a result a number of AAC Flights were formed to supply targets and towed drogues for AA guns, as well as simulating low level and dive bombing attacks on troops and ground installations. By the end of 1941, the flights had expanded to squadron strength, equipped with a range of different aircraft types, and provided detachments to a number of airfields closer to the areas of exercise. These non-operational squadrons were in the ranges of 285 to 291, 516 to 595 and 631 to 695.

Above: **An old Hurricane Mk. I still working in September 1943, in this case helping the Royal Navy. (Paul Anstee)**

287

AAC
SQUADRON

Code Letters:
KZ

Usage:
Mk.I, IIb & IV
Nov 41 to Feb 44

Base:
Croydon 11/41 - Feb 44

288

AAC
SQUADRON

Code Letters:
RP

Usage:
Mk.I & IIc
Nov 41 to Dec 44

Bases:
Digby 11/41 – 12/42
Wellingore 12/42 – 1/43
Digby 1/43 – 11/43
Digby 11/43 – 1/44
Collyweston 1/44 – 11/44

289

AAC
SQUADRON

Code Letters:
YE

Usage:
Mk.I, IIc & IV
Dec 41 to June 45

Bases:
Detling 12/43 – 11/44
Hornchurch 11/44 – 6/45

290

AAC
SQUADRON

Code Letters:
X6

Usage:
Mk.IIc
Dec 43 to Jan 45

Bases:
Newtonards 12/43 – 3/44
Long Kesh 3/44 – 8/44
Turnhouse 8/44 – 1/45

302 SQUADRON

Code Letters:
WX

Usage:
Mk.I
July 40 to Mar 41
May 41 to July 41
Mk.IIa
Mar 41 to May 41
Mk.IIb
July 41 - Oct 41

Bases:
Leconfield 7/40 – 10/40
Northolt 10/40 – 11/40
Westhampnett 11/40 – 4/41
Kenley 4/41 – 5/41
Jurby 5/41 - 8/41
Church Stanton 8/41 – 9/41
Warmwell 9/41 – 10/41

Above: **Five pilots of No. 302 (Polish) Squadron. Szulc, Kratke, Brzezina, Szczesny, and Koscik in front of a Hurricane with the later red and white Polish emblem on the cowl.**

Below: **Bronislaw Malinowski, who flew with No. 43 Squadron in the Battle of Britain, joined 302 in April 1941 and was one of 'Skalski's Circus' in the Western Desert. He survived the war. (ww2images.com)**

Below: **Below: Wlodzimierz Karwowski, one of the first pilots with 302. He later went to No. 316 Squadron and then became CO of No. 306 Squadron. He survived the war and settled in New Zealand. (ww2images.com)**

Below: **Piotr Ostaszewski- Ostoja flew with No. 609 Squadron in the Battle of Britain and served with a number of squadrons. He survived the war and left the RAF with the rank of wing commander in 1946. (ww2images.com)**

303 SQUADRON

Code Letters:

RF

Usage:

Mk.I
Aug 40 to Jan 41
Aug 41 to Oct 41

Bases:

Northolt 8/40 – 10/40
Leconfield 10/40 – 1/41
Northolt 1/41 – 7/41
Speke 7/41 – 10/41

Above: **Hurricane I P3700 of No. 303 Squadron at Northolt in early September 1940. It was shot down on 9 September 1940 its pilot, Flight Sergeant Wunsche, bailing out with burns.**

Left: **Sergeant Josef Frantisek. The Czech 'ace' with No. 303 Squadron was the highest scoring pilot in the Battle of Britain with 17 victories. He was killed on 8 October 1940.**

Right: **Four 303 'aces' with their DFCs. Left to right, Urbanowicz (18 destroyed - survived the war), Zumbach (12 destroyed - survived the war), Feric (8 destroyed - killed 14 February 1942), Henneberg (8 destroyed - killed 12 April 1941).**

Flight Lieutenant J A Kent

'Johnny' Kent from Winnipeg, Canada, learned to fly at 17 and joined the RAF in 1935 at 21. He qualified as a gunner instructor and became a test pilot at Farnborough. In May 1940 he was flying photo-recce missions in unarmed Spitfires. No. 303 Squadron was forming in July and Kent was posted as a flight commander. He destroyed four aircraft during the Battle of Britain, but left to command No. 92 Squadron flying Spitfires in October. He was back at Northolt as Wing Commander Flying in June 1941, then moved to Kenley. The rest of his career was spent in senior posts until his retirement as a Group Captain in 1956.

Above: **Sergeant Eugeniusz Szaposznikow, another of No. 303 Squadron's 'aces'. He is credited with bringing down eight enemy aircraft during the Battle of Britain and survived the war.**

HURRICANES and the BATTLE of BRITAIN

With the expansion in the mid 1930s, the organisation of the RAF had to keep pace with the increase in size to be prepared to combat the expected hostile German intentions. A major step was to bring into being the Commands on a functional, rather than regional, basis and on 14 July 1936 Air Marshall Hugh C T Dowding formed Headquarters Fighter Command at Bentley Priory, near Stanmore in North London.

At the start of the Battle of Britain Fighter Command was organised into four Groups, 11 Group being in the front line with the defence of the South East of England, led by AVM Keith Park. Providing support to 11 Group was12 Group led by AVM Trafford Leigh-Mallory covering the East Coast north of London up to Yorkshire. 10 Group based in the South West of England from Hampshire to Cornwall was lead by AVM Sir Quintin Brand. No. 13 Group was tasked with covering the defence of Northern Britain commanded by AVM Richard Saul and was often used during the Battle for squadrons to retire for rest, re-equipping and re-training before rejoining the Battle in the south. However, it was not all resting in the north of Britain as enemy raids from occupied Norway were countered successfully.

At the opening of the Battle of Britain, No. 11 Group had 21 fighter squadrons at thirteen airfields, of which thirteen were equipped with Hurricanes. Of the remainder, six were equipped with Spitfires and two with the outdated Blenheim. No. 10 Group had nine squadrons at six airfields to defend the western flank of Britain. Three were equipped with Hurricanes, four with Spitfires, one had Blenheims and one had anti-quated Gladiator biplanes. No.12 Group had fourteen squadrons based on nine airfields spread from Duxford in the south to Leconfield in the north with five operating Hurricanes. The remainder consisted of six Spitfire units, two Blenheim, and one with the ineffective and vulnerable Defiant. No.13 group covered the north of England, Scotland and Northern Ireland with twelve squadrons at twelve airfields, eight squadrons operating Hurricanes. In addition there were two Spitfire squadrons and one each with Blenheims and Defiants. The Hurricane had been used almost exclusively in the Battle of France and was still the major type used in the Battle of Britain.

Following the evacuation of Dunkirk on 3 June, there was a welcome but unexplained pause of about a month in the German advances, which allowed the RAF a breathing space to evolve new tactics, train new pilots and replace lost aircraft. A new tactic adopted for the fighters was to operate as a paired unit with the number two covering the leader's tail. At the opening of the Battle, while the RAF had 905 aircraft available for the defence of Britain, there were only 1,103 pilots with the squadrons of which 820 were combat ready, the remainder being under active training. The OTUs were producing about twenty new Hurricane pilots every week on the earlier standard of aircraft, leaving the squadrons to convert the pilots to be able to operate the later versions with reflector gun sight and variable pitch propeller in combat.

Initial German attacks started on 7 July against shipping in the Channel resulting in all major supplies by sea being diverted to western ports rather than London. Although the German Bf109 was a difficult adversary for the Hurricanes, the Bf110 fighter and Ju87 dive bombers were very vulnerable. The Bf109 was usually at the limit of its endurance, allowing only a short period for escort duties to the more vulnerable bombers. The enemy aircraft were operating over hostile territory, so even if pilots survived being shot down, they were soon taken prisoner. The RAF squadron numbers were boosted by the addition of volunteer FAA pilots and the release for combat of the American volunteer pilots, plus the Allied and Commonwealth, Czech, Polish, and Canadian squadrons.

Above: **Having retreated from France, No. 1 Squadron arrived at Northolt in June 1940 as part of 11 Group, with detachments at Hawkinge. In the same month a move was made to Tangmere until August, when the squadron moved back to Northolt. From here there were also detachments to Tangmere, Manston, North Weald and Heathrow. On 9 September 1940 the squadron moved to Wittering in 12 Group for a rest tour, returning to Northolt in December. The first victory claimed in the Battle of Britain was two Bf110s in August. The CO for the Battle was Squadron Leader D A Pemberton.**

Above: **No. 145 Squadron is credited with firing the opening shots of the 'official' Battle of Britain on 8 August when based at Westhampnett. Shortly after it moved to Drem where it remained until the closing days of Battle. During the early days the CO was Squadron Leader John R A Peel.**

The Luftwaffe strategy was to destroy the RAF in the air and on the ground in preparation for an air and sea invasion to be launched in September 1940. The targets included the fighter airfields in an attempt to make them unusable, as well as knocking out the radar chain, which gave warning of impending attacks. Although Reichsmarschall Herman Goering, the Luftwaffe Commander-in-Chief, believed the RAF to be seriously weakened following the Battle of France, there were still enough pilots and fighters to cause significant German losses, with the Luftwaffe manpower about three times that of the RAF.

The first major enemy attack was planned for 13 August with aircraft operating from as far apart as Norway to the Brest Peninsula in an effort to overwhelm the British fighters. But instead of a co-ordinated attack a number of isolated raids developed which still caused major damage with heavy losses on both sides. Thursday 15 August was code named by the Germans *Adler Tag* – Eagle Day, again involving co-ordinated attacks from Scandinavia and the French coastal airfields. The targets were the fighter airfields of both Nos. 10 and 11 Groups being supported by the squadrons in 12 and 13 Groups. The northern raids were by unescorted bombers due to the Bf109 having insufficient range and a number of Ju88 bombers were destroyed by Fighter Command without British losses. On this important day for the Germans, about 70% of Fighter Command's pilots were in action at least once, some units flying up to four combat sorties. Enemy losses were 64 aircraft, with Hurricane pilots claiming 41 victories, although seventeen Hurricanes were shot down for the loss of seven pilots killed and two taken prisoner in France.

No. 17 Squadron was part of 11 Group for the Battle, based at Debden from June 1940. A move to Tangmere came in August and back to Debden in September, where it remained until October. The COs were Squadron Leader C W Williams, who was replaced by Squadron Leader A G Miller in August.

Above: **No. 32 Squadron was in the front line with 11 Group for the Battle, based at Biggin Hill from June until August 1940, before moving to Acklington in 13 Group on 28 August for a rest. 15 August was a busy day for the squadron pilots. They first claimed a Bf109 for the loss of two Hurricanes, later off Selsey Bill three Ju88s and a Do17 were claimed for no loss. Against an attack on Croydon, three more Do17s, a Ju88 and four Bf109s were shot down. During the Battle Squadron Leader J Worrall was CO until replaced by Squadron Leader Crossley DFC in August.**

Above: **No 303 Squadron *Warsaw-Kosciuszko*, was based at Northolt in 11 Group and made its first claim on 30 August. From then until it moved to Leconfield on 11 October it was heavily involved in combat, claiming 117 victories, the highest total of any squadron in the Battle of Britain.**

Above: **From June 1940, No. 85 Squadron was based at Martlesham Heath in 11 Group, with detachments to Castle Camps. A move was made to Debden in August, then to Croydon. Castle Camps was the base for 85 Squadron during September, until a move was made for a rest to Church Fenton in 12 Group. During the Battle, the squadron flew both day and night operations, during August the squadron pilots claimed 44 enemy aircraft destroyed for eight Hurricanes lost and two pilots killed. Squadron Leader Peter Townsend was the CO from May 1940 until June 1941, leading the squadron through the Battle.**

Above: **No. 87 Squadron saw its first action of the Battle on 11 July when four Bf110s destroyed and one probable were claimed. Squadron Leader Lovell-Gregg was CO from July until 15 August when he was shot down and killed. Flight Lieutenant R S Mills DFC took over until December 1940 when Squadron Leader Gleed assumed command.**

This demonstrated conclusively to the German High Command that Fighter Command maintained air superiority despite smaller numbers of aircraft and pilots, and *Adler Tag* was to prove a decisive turning point in the Battle. Serious damage had been inflicted by enemy bombers on airfields, ports and aircraft factories, but Fighter Command had been able to meet all the threats from one end of Britain to the other, disproving the Luftwaffe belief that the RAF fighter defences were concentrated only in southern England.

The decimated Stuka force was withdrawn as too vulnerable with nearly 25% destroyed and the loss of 136 aircrew. In a period of ten days in August, 86 of the slow flying Bf110s with many experienced aircrew had been lost.

Towards the end of August a conflict between Park in 11 Group and Leigh-Mallory in 12 Group came to a head. Whenever the 11 Group airfields to the north of London were under attack, support was requested from 12 Group from the main sector airfield at Duxford. Leigh-Mallory believed his best method of attack was in large numbers with the squadrons formed into wings. It usually took so long for these big wings to get airborne and formed up with a mixture of different performance Hurricanes and Spitfires, that the enemy aircraft were on their way home having done their damage. The wings lacked the desired flexibility, although Leigh-Mallory claimed to be destroying some of the raiders.

Left: **No. 257 (Burma) Squadron became operational on 1 July and claimed its first victory, against a Do17 on 19 July. On 8 August, in a major battle over the Isle of Wight, two enemy aircraft were destroyed and two claimed as damaged for the loss of three pilots. The squadron continued to fight in the Battle of Britain, participating in the defence of London on 15 September when a total of 185 enemy aircraft were destroyed. Operating from Debden, No. 257 Squadron fought over the Thames Estuary, continuing the Battle well into November. On 11 November the squadron claimed eight Italian aircraft destroyed and four more damaged in the only attack by the Italian Air Force over Britain. Squadron Leader T Harkness was the CO from July 1940, until replaced by Squadron Leader Bob Stanford Tuck DFC from October 1940 until July 1941.**

Below: **No. 111 Squadron were responsible for the introduction of the Hurricane into RAF service at their home base of Northolt. At the start of the Battle in June 1940 the squadron was based at Croydon in 11 Group, moving to Debden in August, and back to Croydon in September. On 8 September, the squadron was posted to Drem for a rest tour. During the critical period of the Battle of Britain, Squadron Leader J M Thompson was the CO. Here pilots wait at readiness with Hurricane I, L1822, JU-K and a classy runabout by the caravan.**

During the week commencing 31 August, Fighter Command lost 107 Hurricanes and 71 Spitfires with 55 pilots killed and 78 seriously wounded. This was equivalent to a squadron of pilots and two squadrons of aircraft each day. In the face of superior German numbers, fatigue and the inexperience of replacement pilots was beginning to become critical.

The climax of the Battle came on 7 September, when Goering made the mistake of switching from attacks on airfields to mounting bomber raids on London in an effort to attract every remaining fighter into the air, where they could be destroyed. A total of about 1,000 enemy aircraft were sent against Britain to be met by 21 squadrons (of which fourteen were equipped with Hurricanes) which were launched in defence of the Capital. The Duxford Wing caught up with the enemy bombers after they had unloaded over London Docks and 11 Group fighters faced the enemy formations coming in from the south. At one time there were about 1,250 aircraft in the air, making this one of the largest air battles of the war which lasted just 30 minutes. The final RAF losses for the day were 29 Hurricanes and 15 Spitfires shot down with the loss of 17 pilots, including two squadron commanders and three flight commanders. German losses amounted to 52 aircraft including 26 fighters.

Goering's change of tactics with the bombing of London, often at night, released Fighter Command from defending the airfields and allowed the weary squadrons to be replaced by rested units from the north of Britain. If the German raids on the airfields had continued Fighter Command would not have been able to sustain the casualties at the existing rate. In the first two months of the Battle of Britain, the equivalent of eleven squadrons had been lost, which was greater than the number of new squadrons brought into action since the start of the Battle. Many experienced pilots had been killed or injured and the new pilots lacked the necessary experience to survive. German losses had also been high and the leadership was convinced that Fighter Command was all but destroyed.

On 15 September 1940, now known as Battle of Britain Day, there was another massive attack on London and a rested and restored Fighter Command was able to achieve a resounding victory. For the loss of twenty Hurricanes and seven Spitfires with ten pilots killed, the Luftwaffe lost 36 bombers and 23 fighters, with 163 aircrew either killed or taken prisoner. Fighter Command was obviously still a potent fighting force and the planned invasion of Britain was abandoned until at least the following spring. Fighter Command had held at bay a force superior in numbers and helped to turn the tide of the war in preparation for the Allied invasion of Europe in June 1944.

The air defence of Britain continued until the end of the year with pilots still gaining victories and sustaining losses in the air. It was not until the start of 1941 that the squadrons were able to begin offensive operations over occupied Europe.

Below: **The *Weekend Warriors* of the Royal Auxiliary Air Force made a major contribution to the Battle. Many men were experienced pre-war pilots. No. 601 (County of London Squadron) RAuxAF fought throughout the Battle in southern England. The COs were: Flight Lieutenant, The Hon 'Max' Aitken DFC to 17 July; Squadron Leader Hobson to 10 August; Squadron Leader, The Hon Edward Ward to 19 August; Flight Lieutenant, Sir Archibald Hope for the remainder of the Battle.**

Below: **To keep the pilots in the air as much as possible during the Battle, the ground crews had to work hard to re-arm and refuel the Hurricanes as quickly as possible, often in primitive conditions, and prepare the aircraft for the next sortie. The guns on this aircraft have been fired during its last flight as the fabric patches over the gun ports have been breached.**

306 SQUADRON

Code Letters:
UZ

Usage:
Mk.I
Aug 40 to Apr 41
Mk.IIa
Apr 41 to July 41

Bases:
Church Fenton 8/40 – 11/40
Tern Hill 11/40 – 4/41
Northolt 4/41 – 10/41

Above: **A post Battle of Britain scene with No. 306 Squadron. Note the aircraft carries the red and white chequer emblem used by Polish squadrons later in the war.**

No. 306 Squadron.
The third RAF Polish squadron. It formed at Church Fenton on 28 August 1940 and was declared operational at Tern Hill on 8 November for the defence of the Birmingham area. As well as day sorties, the squadron also flew at night and on 10 May1941 an He111 was shot down at night. In June 1941 the squadron began to convert to Spitfires.

No. 308 Squadron.
This was the fourth Polish day fighter squadron. It formed at Squires Gate on 9 September 1940 but, due to commitment of aircraft to the Battle of Britain, the squadron did not receive the first Hurricanes until November. While still under training the squadron shot down a Ju88 on 24 November and the squadron was declared operational the next month. In February 1941 the squadron began night flying, but did not become a night fighter unit as Spitfires began replacing Hurricanes in March 1941.

Marian Pisarek

Pisarek was born in Poland in 1912 and fought in Poland, shooting down one enemy aircraft. He claimed four more victories with No. 303 Squadron in the Battle of Britain. He spent a few months with No. 315 Squadron, before his posting to No. 308 Squadron as a flight commander and became its CO in June 1941. On 17 April 1942 he became Wing Leader of the Northolt Polish Wing, but was lost just 12 days later when he was shot down by FW190s over the Channel.

308 SQUADRON

Code Letters:
ZF

Usage:
Mk.I
Nov 40 to Apr 41

Bases:
Squires Gate 9/40
Speke 9/40
Baginton 9/40 – 5/41

Below: Hurricane Is of No. 306 (Polish) Squadron. The nearest aircraft is V7118 UZ-V.

310 SQUADRON

Code Letters:
NN

Usage:
Mk.I
July 40 to Mar 41
Mk.IIa
Mar 41 to Dec 41
Mk.IIb
June 41 to Nov 41

Bases:
Duxford 7/40 – 6/41
Martlesham Heath 6/41 – 7/41
Dyce 7/41 – 12/41

Above: **Englishmen with the Czechs, left to right, Flying Officer Boulton, Flight Lieutenant Jeffries DFC and Flight Lieutenant Sinclair. Jeffries fought throughout the Battle of Britain with No. 310 Squadron and became its CO from January to June 1941. He was killed in 1942 when leading No. 106, a Lancaster, Squadron. Boulton died a few days after this photo was taken when he collided with Sinclair's Hurricane near Croydon on 9 September 1940. Sinclair was 'A Flight' Commander and survived the war after commanding several fighter squadrons and holding various staff posts.**

Above: **AVM Leigh-Mallory (AOC 12 Group) at Duxford inspecting the newly formed No. 310 Squadron in July 1940.**

Above: **The Czechoslovakian state lion symbol on the cowling of one of No. 310 Squadron's Mk.Is.**

Below: **P3707 after a crash landing on 29 October 1940 near Duxford. Flight Lieutenant J Maly had collided with Pilot Officer E Fechtner who died when his Hurricane crashed.**

309 SQUADRON

Code Letters:
WC

Usage:
Mk.IIc
Apr 44 to Oct 44

Base:
Drem & Hutton Cranswick
4/44 - 10/44

Right: **Z2770, NN-J undergoing maintenance in one of Duxford's famous hangars in spring 1941.**

No. 310 Squadron formed with Czech personnel at Duxford on 10 July 1940 and was operational on 17 August. The first action was on 26 August with one Bf110 destroyed for the loss of three Hurricanes, although the pilots were safe. The squadron was involved heavily in the Battle of Britain with a total of 37.5 aircraft destroyed by the end of the month. As part of the Duxford Wing, 310 went over to the offensive in February 1941, including some night patrols. The squadron was then involved in coastal patrols until moving to Dyce where it started re-equipping with Spitfires in October 1941.

Below: **Flying Officer K Kimlicka's dog holds his flying helmet for him!**

Below: **Squadron Leader Frantisek Weber, the CO of No. 310 Squadron from June 1941 to April 1942.**

Below: **W9323, a Hurricane Mk.I served first with No.310 Squadron and survived the war with a variety of units before being scrapped in 1946.**

312
SQUADRON

Code Letters:
DU

Usage:
Mk.I
Aug 40 to May 41
Mk.IIb
May 41 to Dec 41

Bases:
Duxford 8/40 – 9/40
Speke 9/40 – 3/41
Valley 3/40 – 4/41
Jurby 4/41 – 5/41
Kenley 5/41 – 7/41
Martlesham Heath 7/41 – 8/41
Ayr 8/41 – 1/42

Above: **No. 312 formed at Duxford on 29 August 1940. In September it was part of the defence of Liverpool, but with little action the squadron flew convoy patrols from January 1941 until moving back to 11 Group in May to fly escort to bombing raids over occupied France. Flying north to Ayr the squadron converted to Spitfires from October 1941.**

Left: **Ju88 M7+DK of 2./KGr806 crash landed at Bromborough, Merseyside after being target practice for No. 302 Squadron pilots F/Lt Gillam, P/O Vasatko and Sgt Stehlik.**

Right: **Hurricanes of No. 312 (Czech) Squadron at Speke in late 1940 beat-up V6935, DU-W. The aircraft went to 56 OTU, but dived into the ground near Sutton Bridge on 16 August 1941.**

Below: **The first production Hurricane I, L1547, was issued to No. 312 (Czech) Squadron at Speke. It was lost on 10 October 1940 when it caught fire in the air and crashed in the Mersey with the death of the pilot, Sergeant O Hanzlicek.**

Right: **Mk. I P3612, DU-N, with the engine running and ready to go in January 1941. Note the 'fifth machine gun port' in each wing and the Czech emblem under the cockpit. This aircraft crashed with the squadron on 22 February 1941 when Sergeant Kruta took off from Penrhos. The pilot was unhurt.**

Right: **Hurricane IIb Z3588, DU-S, of No. 312 Squadron. This Hurricane later served with No. 253 Squadron and was sent to Russia in September 1942. The hand hold in the fuselage side is well illustrated by the man standing at the wing route.**

Below: **Wind-chill at Penrhos in February 1941. The aircraft is P3612 again - the 'ten gun' Hurricane which crashed on take-off days after this picture was taken.**

Below: **V7066 and Flight Lieutenant Dawbarn went missing on 10 April 1941 after combat with a Do17. Behind is a Hawker Henley of No. 9 Bombing and Gunnery School.**

315 SQUADRON

Code Letters:
PK

Usage:
Mk.I
Feb 41 to July 41

Bases:
Acklington 1/41 - 3/41
Speke 3/41 - 7/41
Northolt 7/41 - 4/42

No. 315 (Polish) Squadron
Formed at Acklington on 21 January 1941 from the City of Deblin Squadron of the Polish Air Force with Hurricanes. It was the sixth of the Polish fighter squadrons to be created and became operational on 18 March at Speke, where it was tasked with convoy patrols over the Irish Sea. A move was made south to Northolt in July, by which time the squadron was beginning to re-equip with Spitfires.

In contrast to the many 'Box Brownie' snap shots taken during the war this photographer had time to concentrate on his art. Northolt was the home to many of the Polish squadrons and there is now a memorial close by dedicated to these brave Allied airmen.

No. 316 (Polish) Squadron
The Polish "City of Warsaw" Squadron was formed at Pembrey on 15 February 1941, becoming operational on 25 March. The duties of the squadron were coastal and convoy patrols around the Bristol Channel with the first action on 1 April. From October 1941 Spitfires began to replace the Hurricanes.

No. 317 (Polish) Squadron
The "Wilenski" Squadron formed at Acklington on 22 February 1941 and was operational on East Coast convoy patrols in just over a month. The first victory was on 2 June when a Ju88 was shot down. With the arrival of Hurricane IIs the squadron went on the offensive. In October Spitfires replaced Hurricanes.

No. 318 (Polish) Squadron
Formed at Detling on 20 March 1943 with Polish personnel as a tactical reconnaissance unit, which continued until August when the squadron moved to Egypt. Re-equipped with Hurricane IIs it worked up with the Polish Army, but did not see any action until moving to Italy in May 1944 with Spitfires.

No. 331 (Norwegian) Squadron
Formed at Catterick on 21 July 1941 as the first of the Norwegian fighter squadrons in the RAF, it became operational at Castletown on 15 September 1941. The squadron was involved with defending the Fleet at Scapa Flow, but did not see any action until moving south in May 1942 with Spitfires.

316 SQUADRON

Code Letters:
SZ

Usage:
Mk.I
Feb 41 to July 41
Mk.IIa
July 41 to Oct 41
Mk.IIb
July 41 to Oct 41

Bases:
Pembrey 2/41 – 6/41
Colerne 6/41 – 8/41
Church Stanton 8/41 – 12/41

317 SQUADRON

Code Letters:
JH

Usage:
Mk.I
Feb 41 to July 41
Mk.IIa
July 41 to Oct 41
Mk.IIb
July 41 to Oct 41

Bases:
Acklington 2/41 – 4/41
Ouston 4/41 – 6/41

318 SQUADRON

Code Letters:
LW

Usage:
Mk.I
Mar 43 to Aug 43
Mk.IIb
Sept 43 to Dec 43

Bases:
Detling 3/43 - 8/43
To Egypt 9/43

331 SQUADRON

Code Letters:
FN

Usage:
Mk.I
July 41 to Aug 41
MkIIb
Aug 41 to Dec 41

Bases:
Catterick 7/41 – 8/41
Castletown 8/41 – 9/41
Skeabrae 9/41 – 5/42

401

SQUADRON

Code Letters:

YO

Usage:

Mk.I
Mar 41 to May 41
Mk.IIa
May 41 to Sept 41

Base:

Digby 2/41 – 10/41

Above: **The squadron had formerly been known as No. 1 (RCAF) but, following a move to Digby, it was renumbered No. 401 Squadron on 1 March 1941. Spitfires began to replace the Hurricanes in September 1941. Here Pilot Officer J Small and Sergeant G B Whitney sprint to their Hurricane IIbs during a photo shoot at Digby on 24 July 1941.**

Above: **A daily inspection of the Merlin installation.**

Above: **Faulty brakes being fixed on the port wheel.**

Below: **Ground crew running the Merlin engine on Hurricane IIb Z3658, YO-N, of No. 401 'Ram' Squadron.**

402 SQUADRON

Code Letters:

AE

Usage:

Mk.I
Dec 40 to May 41
Mk.IIa
May 41 to Aug 41
Mk.IIb
Aug 41 to Mar 42

Base:

Digby 12/40 – 5/41
Wellingore 5/41 – 6/41
Martlesham Heath 6/41 – 7/41
Ayr 7/41 – 8/41
Rochford 8/41 – 11/41
Warmwell 11/41 – 3/42

Above: **Hurricane IIb BE485, AE-W, of No. 402 Squadron RCAF. At Rochford the squadron began to work up to the bombing role. The first bombing sortie was on 1 November 1941 against Berck-sur-Mer airfield, pioneering the Hurribomber role with 2 x 250lb bombs.**

Above: **Sergeant Scott displays the 'We Always Deliver' motto to the photographer.**

Above: **The CO, Squadron Leader Morrow DFC at Warmwell early in 1942.**

Below: **A pilot of No. 402 (RCAF) Squadron runs to his aircraft at Digby in this heavily re-touched photo. Originally designated No. 2 Squadron (RCAF) it was formed at Digby on 11 December 1940 from a group of Canadian officers drawn from Nos. 110 and 112 Squadrons (RCAF). The squadron became operational on 28 February 1941 and the following day it was renumbered No. 402 Squadron.**

Above: **Sergeant Handley congratulates Sergeant Robertson at Rochford on 22 September 1941.**

Above: **One of the Mk.IIbs at Warmwell being serviced. The 'erks' are examining the air intake.**

Above: **One of the 'Winnipeg Bears' Hurricanes, this time with 'Butch the Falcon' badge on the cowl.**

Above: **Flight Sergeant R J Emberg and a very Canadian emblem on a cowling.**

Below: **The scene in the crew room at Warmwell on 9 February 1942. The pilots, all sergeants, are from left to right Macklin, Innes, Harmer, Brown, Eady and Hughes.**

438
SQUADRON
2TAF

Code Letters:
F3

Usage:
Mk.IV
Nov43 to Apr 44

Bases:
Digby 11/43 – 12/43
Wittering 12/43 – 1/44
Ayr 1/44 – 3/44
Hurn 3/44 – 4/44
Funtington 4/44 – 6/44

Above: **250 pound bombs being loaded on the rack.**

No. 438 Squadron
Formed on 15 November 1943 by renumbering 118 (BR) Squadron RCAF at Bournemouth it immediately moved to Digby, where the first Hurricane IVs were delivered. With these, the squadron worked up in ground attack duties as part of 143 Wing at Ayr. Typhoons started arriving in March 1944, but the delivery rate was slow and the main equipment was still Hurricanes until April.

No. 439 Squadron
The squadron formed at Bournemouth on 1 January 1944, and moved to Wellingore the same day with Hurricane IVs as an interim equipment before the delivery of Typhoons. With the move to Ayr, the squadron became part of the Canadian 143 Wing, becoming part of the 2nd TAF in March. The heavier armed Typhoons started arriving in March replacing the Hurricanes by April.

No. 440 Squadron
The third RCAF Squadron to form part of a Typhoon Wing in the 2nd TAF was 111 Squadron, which became 440 Squadron at Bournemouth on 1 February 1944. On 13 February it moved to Ayr to become part of 143 Wing with Hurricanes and the first Typhoons. It became operational at Hurn on 28 March by which time Typhoons had replaced the Hurricanes.

Above: **A Canadian LAC inspects a parachute - hope it works!**

439
SQUADRON
2TAF

Code Letters:
5V

Usage:
Mk.IV
Jan 44 to Apr 44

Bases:
Wellingore 1/44
Ayr 1/44 – 3/44
Hurn 3/44 – 4/44

440
SQUADRON
2TAF

Code Letters:
18

Usage:
Mk.IV
Feb 44 to Mar 44

Bases:
Ayr 2/44 – 3/44
Hurn 3/44 – 4/44

486
SQUADRON
RNZAF

Code Letters:
SA

Usage:
Mk.IIb
Mar 42 to July 42

Bases:
Kirton-in-Lindsey 3/42 – 4/42
Wittering 4/42 – 9/42

No. 486 Squadron
This was New Zealand's second fighter squadron in the RAF, the first being the Spitfire equipped No. 485 Squadron. It was formed at Kirton-in-Lindsey on 3 March 1942 and was equipped with Hurricane IIbs for the night fighter role in co-operation with Turbinlite Havocs of 1453 Flight. The squadron became operational on 27 April but with little success the squadron then turned its hand to intruder operations over Europe. Conversion to Typhoons began in July as a day fighter squadron.

501 SQUADRON RAuxAF

Code Letters:
ZH & SD

Usage:
Mk.I
Mar 39 to Apr 41

Bases:
Filton 12/38 – 11/39
Tangmere 11/39 – 5/41
France 5/40 – 6/40
Croydon 6/40 – 7/40
Middle Wallop 7/40
Gravesend 7/40 – 8/40
Kenley 8/40 – 12/40
Filton 12/40 - 4/41

Above: **Hurricane Mk. I, L2124, SD-H of No. 501 Squadron being maintained at Tangmere in September 1939. No. 501 was the first Auxiliary squadron to receive Hurricanes.**

Right: **An early No. 501 Squadron Hurricane I, L1869, after it stalled on landing near Filton during training on 26 March 1939. By 23 August the squadron was operational as part of the defence of Bristol, but in November a move was made to Tangmere and then to France on 10 May in support of the BEF until withdrawing in June.**

Right: **When No. 501 moved, its ground staff were transported by aircraft like this HP42 and Ensign. It re-assembled after the Battle of France at Croydon on 21 June and after building up strength was heavily involved in the Battle of Britain. It returned to its home base at Filton in December. During its time with Hurricanes 501 claimed 149 enemy aircraft destroyed of which 30 had been shot down during the Battle of France. In April 1941 the squadron converted to Spitfires.**

504

SQUADRON RAuxAF

Code Letters:

AW & TM

Usage:

Mk.I
Aug 39 to July 41
Mk.IIb
July 41 to Nov 41

Bases:

Hucknall 10/38 – 9/39
Digby 9/39 – 10/39
Debden 10/39 – 5/40
France 5/40
Wick 5/40 – 6/40
Castletown 6/40 – 9/40
Catterick 9/40
Hendon 9/40
Filton 9/40 – 12/40
Exeter 12/40 – 7/41
Fairwood Common 7/41 – 8/41
Chilbolton 8/41
Ballyhalbert 8/41 – 1/42

Above: **Hurricane P3774 TM-V of No. 504 Squadron at Debden in May 1940 at readiness with the pilot climbing into the cockpit. 504 became a fighter squadron on 31 October 1938 at Hucknall equipped with Gauntlets which it exchanged for Hurricanes in August 1939 for the defence of the Rolls-Royce factories. The squadron was sent to France briefly in May 1940 as part of the BEF reinforcements where there were some losses. The squadron moved to Wick to rebuild ready for a move to Hendon to participate in the Battle of Britain. The Hurricanes were replaced by Spitfires from October 1941.**

Right: **A Hurricane IIb seen in 1941, shortly before the squadron moved on to operate Spitfires.**

Below: **A pre-war group of 504 Squadron officers at Hucknall with two bladed Hurricane Mk. I, AW-O, behind.**

516

SQUADRON

Usage:
Mk.II
Dec 43 to Dec 44

Base:
Dundonald 12/43 - 12/44

Above: **A Hurricane wearing the '5O' codes on No. 521 Met Squadron.**

Above: **Hurricane Mk. XII JS290 of No. 527 Calibration Squadron at Digby. Note the light coloured leading edges of the wings. 527 was formed on 15 June 1943 at Castle Camps as an amalgamation of the various calibration flights in southern England and East Anglia. As the calibration duties reduced, 527 absorbed 528 and 526 Squadrons and was disbanded on 15 April 1946.**

Meteorological Squadrons

Weather has always been a significant factor in the operation of both military and civil aircraft. During wartime the weather conditions over the target area and the proposed route could make the difference between success and failure. In the early days of British military flying, the first flight of the day was the "weather flight" to report on local conditions. In the 1930s this was supplemented by the formation of two Met. Flights equipped with Gauntlets and based at Duxford and Aldergrove. These Flights flew twice daily to 20,000 feet gathering data on temperature, humidity and pressure which was passed via the meteorological organisation to the operational airfields.

With the outbreak of war, this information became vital for operational planning and a number of Flights were formed, later expanding into six squadrons which often flew unarmed over enemy territory, or in hostile weather conditions. The only unit to remain after the war was No. 202 Squadron at Aldergrove which disbanded in July 1964.

518

Met SQUADRON

Usage:
Mk.IIc
Sept 45 to Oct 46

Base:
Aldergrove 9/45 - 10/46

521

Met SQUADRON

Code Letters:
5O

Usage:
Mk.IIc
Aug 44 to Feb 46

Bases:
Docking 9/43 - 10/44
Langham 10/44 - 11/45
Chivenor 11/45 - 4/46

527

Calibration SQUADRON

Code Letters:
WN

Usage:
Mk.I, IIb, XII
June 43 to Apr 45

Bases:
Castle Camps 6/43 – 2/44
Snailwell 2/44 – 4/44
Digby 4/44 – 11/45

The Calibration Squadrons:

The calibration duties included checking communications systems and other radar based equipment, such as blind landing and homing beacons. Initial aircraft used were surplus Lysanders, but as the war progressed many other types of aircraft were operated including some Hurricanes with Nos. 116 and 527 Squadrons.

THE FLYING SEARCHLIGHTS

Before the availability of a practical airborne interception (AI) radar, a number of schemes were tried to detect and destroy enemy aircraft at night. Initially one of the methods was to send up solo Hurricanes in the hope that the pilot could find and destroy an enemy raider by visual contact, but this had very little success. One idea that appeared to have some chance of success was to fit a searchlight in the nose of a relatively large aircraft, which was also fitted with an early AI system, and accompanied by a single-seat fighter. The method was to track the target using the AI and when positioned behind the raider, illuminate it with the light allowing the fighter to move in for the kill.

The technical problem of producing a suitable airborne searchlight was given to the General Electric Company's research laboratories in Wembley. The carbon arc lamp required 1,400 amps at 105 volts, to be provided by state-of-the-art very high discharge batteries which would allow four illuminations of thirty seconds before re-charging at a local power station!

The aircraft most commonly used for this method was a Turbinlite Douglas Havoc converted bomber, accompanied by Hurricanes. The Havocs were fitted with formation keeping lights to assist the "parasite" Hurricane in maintaining contact, the Havoc approaching to within 3,000ft of the target when the code word "hot" was passed to the Hurricane pilot. When the Havoc was positively locked on, the code word "boiling" was passed, when the parasite would drop 300ft and open up to full power ahead of the Havoc. When the Hurricane was about 900ft behind the enemy, the Havoc would turn on the light, illuminating the target for the Hurricane to destroy.

A weakness was once the target was illuminated, it immediately took violent evasive action and was impossible for the Hurricane pilot to follow as he had lost his limited night vision in the brightness of the searchlight. Despite having made a considerable number of contacts with this method, only one enemy aircraft was claimed as destroyed, with one probable and two damaged. The answer was clearly to arm a higher performance aircraft, such as the Beaufighter and Mosquito with AI radar and allow it to shoot down the target itself.

The most powerful light in the world - 50 Megacandles. To focus the light there is a 90cm para-eliptic glass mirror behind the carbon arc lamp.

The Turbinlite Squadrons, Nos. 530 - 539 Squadrons

530 SQUADRON

Operated Hurricane IIc September 1942 - January 1943
Combat base: Hunsdon 5/41 - 1/43
Service history: Formed as 1451 Flt at Hunsdon on 22 May 1941 and became No. 530 Squadron in September 1942 taking over a flight of No. 3 Squadron Hurricanes until disbanding on 25 January 1943.

531 SQUADRON

Operated Hurricane IIc September 1942 - January 1943
Combat bases: West Malling 7/41 - 10/42, Debden 10/42, West Malling 10/42 - 1/43
Service history: On 8 September 1942 after acquiring some of No. 32 Squadron's aircraft 1452 Flt became No. 531 Squadron and disbanded on 31 January 1943.

532 SQUADRON

Operated Hurricane IIc July 1941 - October 1942
Combat bases: Wittering 7/41 - 9/42, Hibaldstow 9/42 - 2/43
Service history: 1453 Flt was renumbered No. 532 Squadron on 4 September 1942 and its final operational patrol was in October 1942, followed by disbandment on 1 February 1943.

533 SQUADRON

Operated Hurricane IIc September 1942 - January 1943
Combat bases: Colerne 7/41 - 1/42, Charmy Down 1/42 - 1/43
Service history: 1454 Flt was renumbered No. 533 Squadron on 8 September 1942 and disbanded on 25 January 1943.

534 SQUADRON

Operated Hurricane IIc September 1942 - January 1943
Combat base: Tangmere 9/42 - 1/43
Service history: 1455 Flt was renumbered No. 534 Squadron on 7 July 1941 and disbanded on 25 January 1943.

537 SQUADRON

Operated Hurricane IIc September 1942 - January 1943
Combat bases: Middle Wallop 9/42 - 1/43
Service history: 1458 Flt was renumbered No. 537 Squadron on 8 September 1942 and disbanded on 25 January 1943.

538 SQUADRON

Operated Hurricane IIc September 1942 - January 1943
Combat bases: Hunsdon 9/41, Hibaldstow 9/41 - 1/43
Service history: 1459 Flt was renumbered No. 538 Squadron on 8 September 1942 and the first victory was an He111 on 30 April. The squadron disbanded on 25 January 1943.

539 SQUADRON

Operated Hurricane IIc September 1942 - January 1943
Combat bases: Acklington 9/42 - 1/43
Service history: 1460 Flt was renumbered No. 539 Squadron on 2 September 1942, but remained operational only until October, and disbanded on 25 January 1943.

Above: **Checking the radio equipment vital for co-operation with the AA units.**

567

AAC SQUADRON

Code Letters:
I4

Usage:
Mk. IIc
Sept 42 to Jan 43

Base:
Acklington 9/42 - 1/43

567 Squadron. Formed on 1 December 1943 from 1624 Flight to provide AAC facilities over Kent and the Thames Estuary until it was disbanded at West Malling on 15 June 1946.

Right: **A Mk. IV straight off the production line. The Anti Aircraft Co-Operation Squadrons used a variety of Hurricane marks passed down from front-line squadrons. By the late stages of the war Mk.IIc and Mk. IVs were to be found in all units. The Hurricanes were used for simulating attacks, Martinets were used for target towing and twin engined aircraft for searchlight and gun laying practice.**

577

AAC SQUADRON

Code Letters:
3Y

Usage:
Mk. IIc, IV
Dec 43 to July 45

Base:
Castle Bromwich 12/43 - 6/46

587

AAC SQUADRON

Code Letters:
M4

Usage:
Mk. IIc, IV
Sept 42 to Jan 43

Bases:
Weston Zoyland 12/43 – 4/44
Culmhead 4/44 – 10/44
Weston Zoyland 10/44 – 6/46

595

AAC SQUADRON

Code Letters:
7B

Usage:
Mk. IIc, IV
Dec 43 to Dec 44

Base:
Aberporth 12/43 - 4/46

577 Squadron. The squadron formed on 1 December 1943 and operated Hurricanes with Spitfires, Oxfords and Beaufighters serving the defences in the Midlands until disbanding on 15 June 1946.

587 Squadron. Formed at Weston Zoyland on 1 December 1943 to provide cover for the defences in the South-West and Bristol Channel areas, the squadron finally disbanded on 15 June 1946 at Tangmere.

595 Squadron. Formed at Aberporth on 1 December 1943 to serve the Welsh region and continued in operation until it was renumbered 5 Squadron on 11 February 1949 at Pembrey.

601

County of London SQUADRON

Code Letters:

UF

Usage:

Mk. I

Feb 40 to Mar 41

Mk.IIb

Mar 41 to Aug 41

Bases:

Tangmere 12/39 – 6/40

Middle Wallop 6/40

Tangmere 6/40 – 8/40

Debden 8/40 – 9/40

Tangmere 9/40

Exeter 9/40 – 12/40

Northolt 12/40 – 5/41

Manston 5/41 – 6/41

Matlaske 6/41 – 8/41

Above: **A group of No. 601 Squadron pilots at Tangmere in 1940 with Squadron Leader Max Aitken DFC, the CO from June to July 1940, is the left of the two on the right.**

William Pancoast Clyde

'Little Billy' Clyde was one of the pre-war adventurers who were in the Auxiliary Air Force. He skied for Britain and, in 1938, left to make a life in Mexico. As soon as war was declared he returned England and joined No. 601 Squadron. On 27 May he made his first combat claim, for two Me110s shot down near Dunkirk, and shot down a Do17 on 6 June. It was on 13 August that he had his most hectic day's air fighting. On his first sortie he probably destroyed a Do17, on his second he destroyed an Me110 and damaged another, finally, on his third sortie of the day he shot down two more Me110s over Hampshire. His final total for the Battle of Britain was nine destroyed, one shared, two probables and two damaged. In October 1940 he took a non-operational job, survived the war and returned to Mexico.

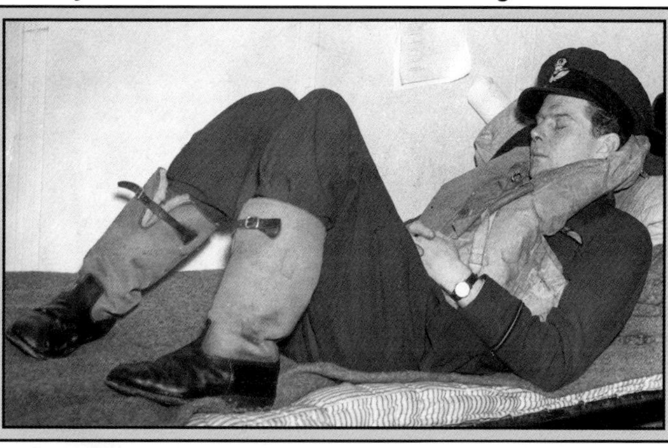

Below: **Refuelling three of No. 601 Squadron's Hurricanes at Tangmere in the early days of the Battle of Britain.**

Above: **Hurricane Mk. I of No. 601 Squadron with Flying Officer Whitney and ground crew. Hurricanes replaced Blenheims in February 1940 and were used as reinforcements in France where the squadron suffered a number of losses.**

Above: **All black Hurricane Mk. IIb of No. 601 Squadron, probably at Manston in 1941.**

The Honourable J W M Aitken

Son of Lord Beaverbrook of newspaper fame and Minister of Aircraft Production, Max joined 601 in 1935. He became its CO in June 1940 and left to take up non-operational duties on July after claiming a total of seven aircraft shot down. He returned to operations later flying Beaufighters and finished the war as CO of the Banff Strike Wing. After the war he was CO of 601, an MP, knighted, and succeeded his father as Lord Beaverbrook.

Below: **A group of pilots from No. 601 Squadron at the end of the Battle of Britain, by which time it had claimed 100 enemy aircraft destroyed and been awarded ten DFCs.**

605

County of Warwick SQUADRON

Code Letters:
UP

Usage:
Mk. I
Aug 39 to Dec 40
Mk.IIa
Nov 40 to Aug 41
Mk. IIb
Aug 41 to Mar 42

Bases:
Tangmere 8/39 – 2/40
Leuchars 2/40
Wick 2/40 – 5/40
Hawkinge 5/40
Drem 5/40 – 9/40
Croydon 9/40 – 2/41
Martlesham Heath 2/41 – 3/41
Tern Hill 3/41 – 5/41
Baginton 5/41 – 9/41
Kenley 9/41 – 10/41
Sealand 10/41 – 12/41
To the Far East

Above: **The replacement of Gladiators by Hurricanes was completed by November 1939 and a move was made to Scotland for the defence of Scapa Flow where the first victory was claimed in April 1940. Moving south, the squadron covered the evacuation of from Dunkirk where there were a number of losses including the CO, Squadron Leader Perry.**

Archie McKellar

The five foot three inch tall Scot, Archibald McKellar, was born in 1912 and joined No. 602 Squadron in 1936. He shared in the destruction of an He111 on 28 October 1939, the first to fall on British soil. In June 1940 he was posted as a flight commander to No. 605 Squadron. In late September he took command of the squadron as Acting Squadron Leader. On 1 November 1940 he was in combat with Me109 south of London and was killed in a crash while attempting to land at Addisham. He was credited with a total of 17 aircraft destroyed, three shared, five probables and three more aircraft damaged.

Below: **Maintaining the Brownings. After participating in the Battle of France with Gladiators, 607 squadron re-equipped with Hurricanes at Usworth, going into operation on 15 August claiming eight destroyed, six probables and five damaged out of a force of 40 - 60 He.111s and Do.17s. The squadron flew its first action as part of the Tangmere Wing on 8 September, but returned north to fly convoy patrols and train Polish pilots.**

607

County of Durham SQUADRON

Code Letters:
AF

Usage:
Mk. I
June 40 to June 41
Mk.IIa
June 41 to Aug 41
Mk. IIb
July 41 to Mar 42
Mk.IIc
June 42 to Feb 43

Bases:
Usworth 6/40 – 9/40
Tangmere 9/40 – 10/40
Turnhouse 10/40 – 11/40
Drem 11/40 – 12/40
Usworth 12/40 – 1/41
Macmerry 1/41 – 3/41
Drem 3/41 – 4/41
Skitten 4/41 – 7/41
Castletown 7/41 – 8/41
Martlesham Heath 8/41 – 10/41
Manston 10/41 – 3/42
To India

Left: **Pilot Officer Millard on the nose of Hurricane KW-J of No. 615 Squadron. (J G P Millard)**

Battle of Britain Pilot

Jocelyn George Power Millard, known as Milly in the RAF and Joce to his friends, enlisted in the RAFVR in August 1937 whilst working at de Havilland Aircraft at Hatfield, whom he had joined in 1934. The RAFVR provided the benefit of combining both an engineering and flying career. His initial and advanced flying training was done at No.1 E&RFTS (Elementary & Reserve Flying Training School) at Hatfield, which de Havilland operated on behalf of the RAF. The initial part of the training, referred to as the ab initio course, was 50 hours on Tiger Moths followed by advanced training on the Hawker biplane variants, such as the Hart, Audax and Hind.

On 1 September 1939 he received a letter notifying him that he had been mobilised into the RAF and to wait instructions. A few weeks later he was posted to Prestwick in Scotland for a flying instructor's course, which finished in November. After this he heard nothing until March 1940 when he was posted to 9 FTS (Flying Training School) at Ansty near Coventry for an 'Advanced Elementary' course, at the end of which he was assessed as an above average pilot.

Joce was then posted to 12 SFTS (Service FTS) at Grantham, which was equipped with Ansons and Battles. He began the course on Ansons which dismayed him and realised that he could never have any enthusiasm for flying this type, especially when others on the course were on Battles, he asked for a transfer to the Battle Flight. In an interview with the squadron commander he explained that he would not be able to give his best if he remained on Ansons. His transfer to Battles was granted, but he was told that by the end of the course he would be expected to have justified his request. After a mid course progress test by the flight commander, he was assessed as an above average pilot and an above average pilot-navigator. At the end of the course in August 1940, he was top in ground subjects and his final test was waived, with a further assessment as an above average pilot and commissioned as a pilot officer.

From Grantham he was posted to 1 SAC (School of Army Co-operation) at Old Sarum in Wiltshire which was equipped with Lysanders and Hectors. He found that all flying activities there were Army related and, having no desire to fly with or for the Army, persevered with a request for a posting to Fighter Command.

Given the choice of a Spitfire or Hurricane OTU, and bearing in mind the recommendation of a school friend who was with 73 Squadron at the time, he chose the Hurricane 6 OTU at Sutton Bridge. Having spent the previous six months flying Battles, all that was required before his first flight in a Hurricane was a circuit in a Harvard. The Hurricanes at the OTU were primitive in several respects - two-blade fixed pitch wooden propeller, a ring and bead gun-sight and a very unsatisfactory hydraulic system for undercarriage operation, but primitive as they were, they were faster than any other aircraft he had flown.

After about ten hours at 6 OTU which included circuits and landings, practice forced landings, combat tactics and formation flying, Joce was posted to No. 1 Squadron at Wittering. The station commander was Wing Commander Harry Broadhurst, and the CO, Squadron Leader Pemberton, who was later killed in a flying accident. Wing Co. Harry Broadhurst, when CO of No. 111 Squadron at Acklington, claimed the first victory of the air war when he shot down an He111 into the sea off Newcastle on 29 November 1939.

Unlike the primitive aircraft at the OTU, those on the squadron were to operational standard, having several important features such as a reflector gun sight, a variable pitch propeller and an improved undercarriage system making the aircraft a vast improvement from those used on training. At the time, the movement of pilots from one squadron to another was quite frequent with postings from one to another squadron in turn. After about a month with No. 1 Squadron, he was posted to No. 242 Squadron at Coltishall, commanded by Squadron Leader Douglas Bader. Bader explained that although 242 was an RAF squadron, it was supposed to consist of all Canadian pilots and consequently at a later date there might be an exchange. Following a move by No. 242 Squadron to Duxford, Joce was posted a few weeks later to No. 615 Squadron at Northolt in exchange for a Canadian pilot posted to 242.

In December 1940, No. 615 Squadron moved to Kenley. Although the air battles of 15 September brought an end to the threat of invasion, and the Battle of Britain officially ended on 31 October, for the rest of the year and into the early months of 1941, there was still a considerable amount of aerial activity. This resulted in the continuing loss of life and aircraft to both sides. During this period, 615 and the other squadrons were busy with interceptions, regular sector patrols and escorting shipping in the Channel.

Below: **Pilot Officer Jocelyn Millard who served with Nos. 1, 242 and 615 Squadrons flying Hurricanes from August 1940 to March 1941. (J G P Millard)**

Above: **The 615 Squadron pilots pose with the squadron mascot by a Hurricane at Northolt. (J G P Millard)**

In February 1941 the squadron was equipped with the far superior Hurricane Mk.IIbs. They retained the good handling qualities of their predecessors, but were fitted with a Merlin XX engine capable of a maximum of 13lb of boost in emergency, a two-stage supercharger and twelve machine guns. The new engine allowed the aircraft to reach a ceiling of over 30,000ft, some 10,000ft in excess of that reached by earlier versions.

The early months of 1941 saw a further lessening of enemy aircraft activity and 615 together with other squadrons was switched to offensive roles. Examples were Rhubarbs - a small scale fighter or fighter-bomber attack on ground targets of opportunity; Sweeps - an offensive formation comprising fighters or fighters and bombers to draw the enemy; and escorting Blenheims on bombing raids.

Below: **A typical squadron briefing at Northolt with pilots allocated to Hurricanes by the side letter. (J G P Millard)**

On the morning of 1 March 1941, No. 615 Squadron was scrambled on two occasions to patrol at 30,000ft over Dungeness and each time were recalled to base thirty minutes after take-off. The second recall brought to an end his time with Fighter Command, as after landing he was informed that he was being posted to the CFS at Upavon. Of the Hurricane, he said it was a wonderful aircraft to fly, and a war-horse, which he felt to be 'impregnable' and in which he felt safe.

In April, after having successfully completed the CFS course on single and twin engine aircraft, he was posted to the Royal Air Force College at Cranwell as a flying instructor on Oxford twin engine advanced trainers. In the following July a posting was made to 35 SFTS in Canada, where he remained until its closure in February 1944. At 35 SFTS, he was in turn flying instructor, flight commander and following the upgrading of his Instructor's Category to A2 by the Visiting Flight of the RCAF CFS, he was appointed Examining Officer with the role of assessing flying instructors and subsequently became Squadron Commander. With the upgrading of his category to A2, the Visiting Flight assessed him as an above average pilot and instructor and on closure of 35 SFTS a year later, the assessment was repeated.

On return to Britain, Joce was posted to Technical Training Command in which he flew Dominies at the Radio School at Yatesbury for eighteen months. At the end of this period the war in Europe had finished, bringing an end to all aircrew training. Being in the General Duties Branch of the RAF, he was then transferred to administrative duties, his final rating for flying ability being recorded as above average as a pilot and staff pilot. Finding administrative duties frustrating and with little hope or opportunity of being able to return to flying duties, after much deliberation, he decided to leave the service.

He joined the newly formed Ministry of Civil Aviation (MCA) as an operations officer, in which capacity he was able to continue a flying career. After five years with the MCA he rejoined de Havilland, where he remained for eleven years before joining the Ministry of Defence, from which he retired in 1980. Joce, now 87 years of age, lives in Letchworth and is one of the surviving members of 'The Few'.

615

County of Surrey SQUADRON

Code Letters:

KW

Usage:

Mk.I
Apr 40 to Feb 41
Apr to July 41
Mk.IIa
Feb 41 to Apr 41
Mk.IIb
July 41 to Mar 42
Mk.IIc
July 41 to Mar 42
June 42 to Sept 43

Bases:

France 11/39 – 5/40
Kenley 5/40 – 8/40
Prestwick 8/40 – 10/40
Northolt 10/40 – 12/40
Kenley 12/40 – 4/41
Valley 4/41 – 9/41
Manston 9/41 – 11/41
Angle 11/41 – 1/42
Fairwood Common 1/42 – 3/42
To India

Above: **Hurricane Mk. IIa Z2703 KW-M of No. 615 Squadron at Kenley in February 1941. This aircraft was presented by the people of Croydon and ended its life in Russia.**

Left: **No. 615 Squadron Hurricanes dispersed at Northolt with some of the aircrew. (J G P Millard)**

Below: **No. 610 Squadron's first Hurricanes were delivered on 5 September 1939, but after three weeks they were transferred to No. 605 Squadron and on 30 September Spitfires began to arrive.**

610

County of Chester SQUADRON

Code Letters:

JE

Usage:

Mk.I
Sept 39

Base:

Hooton Park 1/39 to 10/39

Above: **Hurricane Mk.Is of 615 Squadron landing at Northolt in October 1940.**

Left: **Aircrew and ground crew of No. 615 Squadron relax on Hurricane IIa KW-F at Valley, from where shipping patrols were flown. The squadron embarked for India starting offensive operations on 5 December 1942 and continued with Spitfires replacing the Hurricanes from September 1943.**

Left: **Churchill was invited to become No. 615 Squadron's Honorary Air Commodore in 1938 and it became known as 'Churchill's Own'. Here is seen visiting in September 1941.**

As part of the BEF No. 615 Squadron converted from Gladiators to Hurricanes from April 1940 ready to take part in the Battle of France. After return of the remains of the squadron to Kenley in May 1940 the squadron was ready for the Battle of Britain, but when further depleted retired to Prestwick to rebuild.

Above: **A Mk. IIc as used to simulate low level attacks.**

Below: **Typical flying kit of the Hurricane pilot.**

631

AAC SQUADRON

Code Letters: 6D

Usage: Mk. IIc, Mar 44 to July 45

Bases:
Towyn 12/43 - 5/45
Llanbedr 5/45 - 2/49

631 Squadron
Formed on 1 December 1943 to serve the Welsh gunnery ranges until renumbered 20 Squadron.

639

AAC SQUADRON

Usage: Mk. IIc, IV, Aug 44 to Apr 45

Base: Cleave 12/43 - 4/45

639 Squadron
Formed on 1 December 1943 for operations in the Cornish area until disbanding on 30 April 1945.

667

AAC SQUADRON

Code Letters: U4

Usage: Mk. I, IIc, Apr 44 to Aug 45

Base: Gosport 12/43 - 12/45

667 Squadron
Formed on 1 December 1943 and operated fleet co-operation duties until disbanded.

679

AAC SQUADRON

Code Letters: 3M

Usage: Mk. IIc, IV, Dec 43 to June 45

Base: Ipswich 12/43 - 6/45

679 Squadron
Formed on 1 December 1943 to serve East Anglia until 26 June 1945 when it was disbanded.

691

AAC SQUADRON

Code Letters: 5S

Usage: Mk. I, IIc, Dec 43 to Aug 45

Base:
Roborough 12/43 - 2/45
Harrowbeer 2/45 - 8/45

691 Squadron
Formed on 1 December 1943 to serve the Devon and Cornwall areas until renumbered 17 Sqn.

695

AAC SQUADRON

Code Letters: 4M

Usage: Mk. IIc, Dec 43 to Sept 45

Base:
Bircham Newton 12/43 - 8/45
Horsham St. Faith 8/45 - 2/49

695 Squadron
Formed on 1 December 1943 for duties in the Norfolk area until it was renumbered 34 Squadron.

Squadrons / Codes

1	NA & JX	287	KZ
3	OP & QO	288	RP
17	UV & YB	289	YE
32	KT & GZ	290	X6
43	NQ & FT	302	WX
46	RJ & PO	303	RF
56	LR & US	306	UZ
63	UB	308	ZF
71	XR	309	WC
73	HV & TP	310	NN
79	AL & NV	312	DU
81	F	315	PK
85	NO & VY	316	SZ
87	PD & LK	317	JH
96	ZJ	318	LW
98	-	331	FN
111	TM & JU	401	YO
116	II	402	AE
112	AV	438	F3
133	MD	439	5V
134	G	440	18
137	SF	486	SA
145	SO	501	ZH & SD
151	GG & DZ	504	AW & TM
164	FJ	516	-
174	XP	518	-
175	HH	521	5O
181	EL	527	WN
182	XM	530	-
183	HF	531	-
184	BR	532	-
186	AP	533	-
213	AK	534	-
229	RE & HB	537	-
232	EF	538	-
238	VK & KC	539	-
239	HB	567	I4
242	LE	577	3Y
245	DX & MR	587	M4
247	HP & ZY	595	7B
249	GN	601	UF
253	SW	605	UP
255	YD	607	AF
257	DT & FM	610	JE
258	ER	615	KW
260	HS	631	6D
263	HE	639	-
276	AQ	667	U4
279	OS	679	3M
285	VG	691	5S
286	NW	695	4M

Below: **No trouble with this code, 'YO' being No. 401 (RCAF) Squadron at Digby in July 1941.**

Codes / Squadrons

18	440	HB	239	RF	303
53	81	HE	263	RJ	46
3M	679	HF	183	RP	288
3Y	577	HH	175	SA	486
4M	695	HP	247	SD	501
5O	521	HS	260	SF	137
5S	691	HV	73	SO	145
5V	439	I4	567	SW	253
6D	631	II	116	SZ	316
7B	595	JE	610	TM	111
AE	402	JH	317	TM	504
AF	607	JU	111	TP	73
AK	213	JX	1	U4	667
AL	79	KC	238	UB	63
AP	186	KT	32	UF	601
AQ	276	KW	615	UP	605
AV	112	KZ	287	US	56
AW	504	LE	242	UV	17
BR	184	LK	87	UZ	306
DT	257	LR	56	VG	285
DU	312	LW	318	VK	238
DX	245	M4	587	VY	85
DZ	151	MD	133	WC	309
EF	232	MR	245	WN	527
EL	181	NA	1	WX	302
F3	438	NN	310	X6	290
FJ	164	NO	85	XM	182
FM	257	NQ	43	XP	174
FN	331	NV	79	XR	71
FT	43	NW	286	YB	17
GG	151	OP	3	YD	255
GN	249	OS	279	YE	289
GQ	134	PD	87	YO	401
GZ	32	PK	315	ZF	308
GZ	134	PO	46	ZH	501
HB	229	QO	3	ZJ	96
		RE	229	ZY	247

Below: **An unusual view of the 'PO' codes worn by No. 46 Squadron in May 1940. The black and white undersides are well displayed here .**

Production Batches

UK Production
K5083 *Prototype*
L1547 - L2146 *600 Hawker built Mk.Is*
N2318 - N2367, N2380 - N2409, N2422 - N2441, N2453 - N2502, N2520 - N2559, N2582 - N2631, N2645 - N2729
300 Hawker built Mk.Is
P2535 - P2584, P2614 - P2653, P2672 - P2701, P2713 - P2732, P2751 - P2770, P2792 - P2836, P2854 - P2888, P2900 - P2924, P2946 - P2995, P3030 - P3069, P3080 - P3124, P3140 - P3179, P3200 - P3234, P3250 - P3264 *500 Gloster Built Mk.Is*
P3265 - P3279, P3300 - P3324, P3345 - P3364, P3380 - P3429, P3348 - P3492, P3515 - P3554, P3574 - P3623, P3640 - P3684, P3700 - P3739, P3755 - P3789, P3802 - P3836, P3854 - P3903, P3920 - P3944, P3960 - P3984, P8809 - P8818, R2680 - R2689, T9519 - T9538, W6667 - W6670 *500 Hawker built Mk.Is, plus 44 attrition replacements.*
R4074 - R4123, R4171 - R4200, R4213 - R4132
100 Gloster built Mk.Is
V6533 - V6582, V6600 - V6649, V6665 - V6704, V6722 - V6761, V6776 - V6825, V6840 - V6889, V6913 - V6962, V6979 - V7028, V7042 - V7081, V7099 - V7138, V7156 - V7195.
500 Gloster built Mk.Is
V7200 - V7209, V7221 - V7260, V7276 - V7318, V7337 - V7386, V7400 - V7446, V7461 - V7510, V7533 - V7572, V7588 - V7627, V7644 - V7690, V7705 - V7737, V7741 - V7780, V7795 - V7838, V7851 - V7862, AS987 - AS990. *500 Hawker built Mk.Is*
W9110 - W9159, W9170 - W9209, W9215 - W9244, W9260 -W9279, W9290 - W9329, W9340 - W9359.
200 Gloster built Mk.Is
Z2308 - Z2357, Z2382 - Z2426, Z2446 - Z2465, Z2479 - Z2528, Z2560 - Z2594, Z2624 - Z2643, Z2661 - Z2705, Z2741 - Z2775, Z2791 - Z2840, Z2882 - Z2931, Z2959 - Z2999, Z3017 - Z3036, Z3050 - Z3099, Z3143 - Z3187, Z3221 - Z3276, Z3310 - Z3359, Z3385 - Z3404, Z3421 - Z3470, Z3489 - Z3523, Z3554 - Z3598, Z3642 - Z3691, Z3740 - Z3784, Z3826 - Z3845, Z3885 - Z3919, Z3969 -Z4018. *1,000 hawker built Mk.IIs*
Z4022 - Z4071, Z4085 - Z4119, Z4161 - Z4205, Z4223 - Z4272, Z4308 - Z4372, Z4347 - Z4391, Z4415 - Z4434, Z4482 - Z4516, Z4532 - Z4581, Z4603 - Z4652. *400 Gloster built Mk.Is*
Z4686 - Z4720, Z4760 - Z4809, Z4832 - Z4876, Z4920 - Z4969, Z4987 - Z5006, Z5038 - Z5097, Z5117 - Z5161, Z5202 - Z5236, Z5252 - Z5271, Z5302 - Z5351, Z5376 - Z5395, Z5434 - Z5483, Z5529 - Z5563, Z5580 - Z5629, Z5649 - Z5693.
600 Gloster built Mk.IIa/IIb

Below: **Hurricane fuselage production line showing the wooden rear fuselage structure ready for fabric covering. (Philip Birtles collection)**

Above: **An early production Hurricane Mk.I with the early tubular metal frame and rear fuselage wooden fairing.**

AP516 - AP550, AP654 - AP613, AP629 - AP648, AP670 - AP714, AP732 - AP781, AP801 - AP825, AP849 - AP898, AP912 - AP936.
300 Austin built Mk.IIs
BG674 - BG723, BG737 - BG771, BG783 - BG832, BG844 - BG888, BG901 - BG920, BG933 - BG977, BG990 - BG999, BH115 - BH154, BH167 - BH201, BH215 - BH264, BH277 - BH296, BH312 - BH361. *450 Gloster built Mk.IIa/IIb/IIc*
BD696 - BD745, BD759 - BD793, BD818 - BD837, BD855 - BD899, BD914 - BD963, BD980 - BD986, BE105 - BE117, BE130 - BE174, BE193 - BE242, BE274 - BE308, BE323 - BE372, BE394 - BE428, BE468 - BE517, BE546 - BE590, BE632 - BE651, BE667 - BE716, BM898 - BM936, BM947 - BM996, BN103 - BN142, BN155 - BN189, BN203 - BN242, BN265 - BN298, BN311 - BN337, BN346 - BN389, BN399 - BN435, BN449 - BN497, BN512 - BN547, BN559 - BN603, BN624 - BN654, BN667 - BN705, BN719 - BN759, BN773 - BN802, BN818 - BN846, BN859 - BN882, BN896 - BN940, BN953 - BN987.
1,350 Hawker built Mk.IIs
BN988 - BN992, BP109 - BP141, BP154 - BP200, BP217 - BP245, BP259 - BP302, BP316 - BP362, BP378 - BP416, BP430 - BP479, BP493 - BP526, BP538 - BP566, BP579 - BP614, BP628 - BP675, BP692 - BP711, BP734 - BP772, HL544 - HL591, HL603 - HL634, HL654 - HL683, HL698 - HL747, HL767 - HL809, HL828 - HL867, HL879 - HL913, HL925 - HL941, HL953 - HL997, HM110 - HM157, HV275 - HV317, HV333 - HV370, HV396 - HV445, HV468 - HV516, HV534 - HV560, HV577 - HV612, HV634 - HV674, HV696 - HV745, HV768 - HV799, HV815 - HV858, HV873 - HV921, HV943 - HV989, HW115 - HW146, HW167 - HW207, HW229 - HW278, HW291 - HW323, HW345 - HW373, HW399 - HW444, HW467 - HW501, HW533 - HW572, HW596 - HW624, HW651 - HW686, HW713 - HW757, HW779 - HW808, HW834 - HW881.
1,888 Hawker built Mk.IIs
KW745 - KW777, KW791 - KW832, KW846 - KW881, KW893 - KW936, KW949 - KW982, KX101 - KX146, KX162 - KX621, KX691 - KX736, KX749 - KX784, KX796 - KX838, KX851 - KX892, KX922 - KX967, KZ111 - KZ156, KZ169 - KZ201, KZ216 - KZ250, KZ266 - KZ301, KZ319 - KZ356, KZ370 - KZ412, KZ424 - KZ470, KZ483 - KZ526, KZ540 - KZ582, KZ597 - KZ612, plus NF668 - NF703 *Sea Hurricane IIc conversions. 1,200 Hawker built MkIIs & Mk.IVs*
KZ613 - KZ632, KZ646 - KZ689, KZ702 - KZ750, KZ766 - KZ801, KZ817 - KZ862, KZ877 - KZ920, KZ933 - KZ949, LA101 -LA144, LB542 - LB575, LB588 - LB624, LB639 - LB687, LB707 - LB744, LB769 - LB801, LB827 - LB862, LB873 - LB913, LB927 - LB973,

Above: **The wing centre-section with the retractable main undercarriage and a pair of fuel tanks being inspected before joining the assembly line.**

LB986 - LB999, LD100 - LD131, LD157 - LD185, LD199 - LD219, LD232 - LD266, LD287 - LD315, LD334 - LD351, LD369 - LD416, LD435 - LD470, LD487 - LD508, LD524 - LD539, LD557 - LD580, LD594 - LD632, LD651 - LD695, LD723 - LD749, LD772 - LD809, LD827 - LD866, LD885 - LD905, LD931 - LD979, LD993 - LD999. *1,205 Hawker built Mk.IIs & Mk.IVs*
LE121 - LE146, LE163 - LE183, LE201 - LE214, LE247 - LE273, LE291 - LE309, LE334 - LE368, LE387 - LE405, LE432 - LE449, LE456 - LE484, LE499 - LE535, LE552 - LE593, LE617 - LE665, LE679 - LE713, LE737 - LE769, LE784 - LE816, LE829 - LE867, LE885 - LE925, LE938 - LE966, LE979 - LE999, LF101 - LF135, LF153 - LF184, LF197 - LF237, LF256 - LF298, LF313 - LF346, LF359 - LF405, LF418 - LF435, LF451 - LF482, LF494 - LF516, LF529 - LF542, LF559 - LF601, LF620 - LF660, LF674 - LF721, LF737 - LF774, MW335 - MW373, PG425 - PG456, PG469 - PG499, PG512 - PG554, PG567 - PG610, PZ730 - PZ778, PZ791 - PZ835, PZ848 - PZ865. *1,357 Hawker built Mk.IIs & Mk.IVs*
NL255 *one Hawker built Mk.V prototype*
Total UK production - 12,952

Canadian Production
P5170 - P5209, T9519 - T9538, Z6983 - Z7017, Z7409 - Z7093, Z7143 - Z7162. 160 *Canadian Car & Foundry built Mk.Is*
AE958 - AE977, AF945 - AF999, AG100 - AG344, AG665 - AG684. *340 Canadian Car & Foundry built Mk.Xs*
AM270 - AM369, AP138. *100 Canadian Car & Foundry built Mk.Xs*
BW835 - BW884. *50 Canadian Car & Foundry built Mk.XIIas*
BW885 - BW999, BX100 - BX134.
150 Canadian Car & Foundry built Mk.XIs
JS219 - JS371, JS374 - JS468.
248 Canadian Car & Foundry built Mk.XIs & Mk.XIIs
PJ660 - PJ695, PJ711 - PJ758, PJ779 - PJ813, PJ842 - PJ872.
150 Canadian Car & Foundry built Mk.XIIs
5376 - 5775. *200 Canadian Car & Foundry built Mk.XIIs*
Total Canadian production - 1,398

Total combined production - 14,350 Hurricanes.

Below: **Hurricane Mk.II final assembly at Langley fitted with four 20mm cannons in the wings.**